Cottage Gardens

Right Morning light falls on one of the many narrow paths at East Lambrook Manor Gardens in Somerset.

Cottage Gardens

A celebration of Britain's most beautiful cottage gardens,
with advice on making your own

Claire Masset

National Trust

First published in the United Kingdom in 2020 by
National Trust Books
43 Great Ormond Street
London
WC1N 3HZ

An imprint of Pavilion Books Group Ltd

ISBN: 9781911358923

A CIP catalogue record for this book is available from the British Library.

10 9 8 7 6 5 4 3 2 1

Reproduction by Rival Colour Ltd, UK
Printed and bound by Toppan Leefung Printing Ltd, China

This book is available at National Trust shops and online at www.nationaltrustbooks.co.uk, or try the publisher (www.pavilionbooks.com) or your local bookshop.

Right Hardy geraniums add a touch of colour to the grey timbers of Little Moreton Hall, Cheshire. **Overleaf** Swathes of *Gladiolus communis* subsp. *byzantinus* are an early summer hallmark at East Lambrook Manor Gardens in Somerset.

Contents

CHAPTER I

INTRODUCTION

Picture a thatched cottage on a beautiful summer's day. A rustic gate stands half-open, beckoning you into the front garden. In this small plot, a jumble of flowers happily grows next to rows of vegetables and fruit bushes. Wigwams of sweet peas and tall hollyhocks tower over the carrots and cabbages. As you reach the cottage door, you are greeted with the most charming of sights: an arbour covered in sweetly scented roses.

This is what springs to mind when I imagine a cottage garden. We all have our own version. Yours might be a red-brick cottage surrounded by delphiniums, lupins and daisies. Someone else's might include an old apple tree in bloom, underplanted with tulips and forget-me-nots. Each of these visions has its roots in the Victorian era, when artists perpetuated a sentimental view of rural life through evocative watercolours of English villages.

But the cottage garden is more than this romanticised interpretation. Its rich history goes back to the medieval cottager's plot. Over the centuries it has been a place of sustenance, a haven for plants on the verge of extinction, and an inspiration for designers of much grander gardens. People from all walks of life have been drawn to it – from poor workers and writers, to intellectuals and aristocrats. It now represents the quintessential English garden style, favoured by gardeners around the world.

As a concept it is hard to define, but you immediately recognise it when you see it. Cosy, snug, informal, profuse, the cottage garden looks entirely at home in its surroundings, as though it has slowly evolved over time – and often it has. Flowers are the stars of the show, but shrubs and topiary usually add a little structure. The cottage garden is marked by modesty. It never tries too hard to impress, for its charm lies in its homeliness.

Left The classic cottage garden, with its rose arch, simple path and mingled planting.
Above *By the Cottage Gate* by Helen Allingham, a typically sentimental portrayal of the Victorian cottage garden.

Above Many of the flowers in this front garden, such as the poppies and the red valerian by the fence, may well have seeded themselves.

In 1893, the editor of *Cottage Gardening* magazine attempted his own interpretation: 'The term is one of which it is impossible to give a definition on hard and fast lines. It cannot be confined to one class of people, because many gentlemen and ladies live in cottages … We should say that a very good rule is that a cottage garden should be one in which all the labour is done by the occupier.' It was exactly this last point that made it appealing to so many, at a time when paid gardening staff were starting to become less common. By the end of the Second World War very few homeowners could afford a full- or even part-time gardener.

The cottage garden style can be adapted to any garden, whether rural or not, small or large. Best of all, it allows for great amounts of self-expression; there are very few rules other than a profusion of plants, a love of flowers and a distinct lack of grandiosity. It is within everyone's reach and ideal for time-poor gardeners with small plots. Even a patio or window box can become a little piece of cottage garden heaven. As William Robinson advised: 'Just be good to your plot, make it fertile and let the flowers tell their story to the heart.' It really is that simple.

Above left Buddleja is one of the easiest shrubs to grow and will reward you with plenty of fragrant blooms from mid- to late summer. **Above right** Hollyhocks growing at Hardy's Cottage in Dorset. **Overleaf** Moss roses and hardy geraniums in the front garden at Hardy's Cottage.

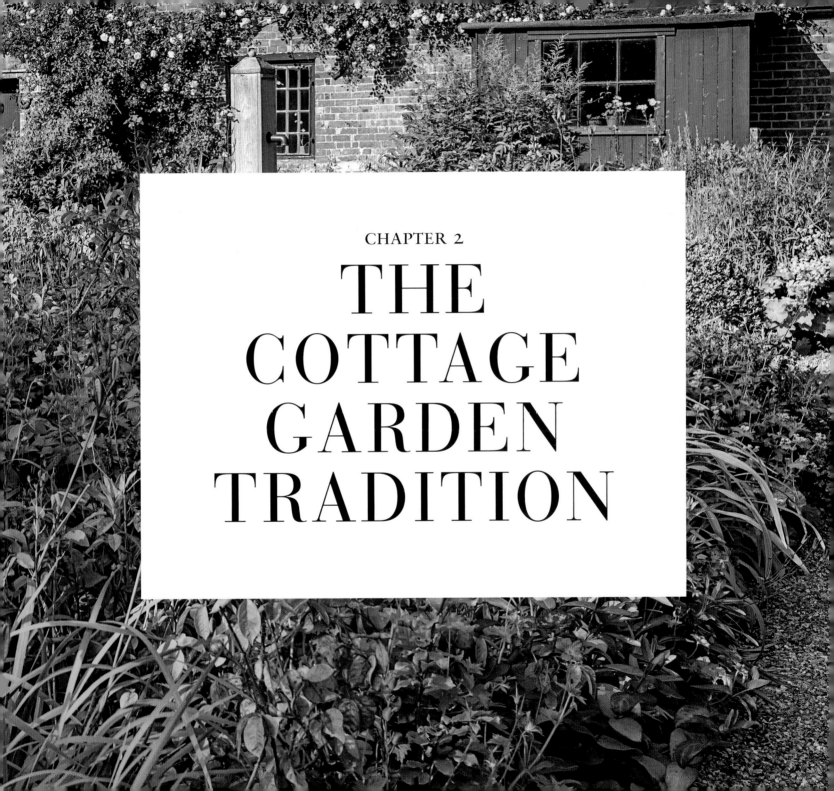

CHAPTER 2

THE COTTAGE GARDEN TRADITION

A plot of one's own

The word cottage comes from the Old English term 'cottar', meaning farm labourer or tenant. In return for work on the land, the cottar was given the lease of a house and a small piece of land. His plot was a place of utility. Beauty, if there was any, was a happy by-product.

Peas, beans, leeks, onions, cabbages and carrots constituted the bulk of the cottager's diet, cooked in a stew known as pottage. Commonly used to flavour ale and food, herbs were widely grown and a main ingredient in home remedies. Borage, for instance, was used as an anti-depressant; comfrey was known to heal wounds; while betony seems to have been a bit of a cure-all, helping with anything from snake and dog bites to arthritis, gout and even drunkenness. Herbal knowledge was passed down from one generation to the next, based as much on lore as on scientific fact. Rosemary, handy for headaches, colds and nervous diseases, was grown near the entrance to the cottage to ward off witches. Vervain, if planted in the garden, could help you attract a lover, for whom, once ensnared, you could concoct an aphrodisiac using the same plant.

Aromatic herbs were, of course, also valued for their scent. Mint and meadowsweet were mixed with rushes and strewn on the floor to cover up the many unsavoury odours of the cottage, where animals would frequently share the living space. Lavender and tansy were hung in bunches to repel the inevitable fleas, lice and ticks.

Opposite Meadowsweet or 'the Queene of Medowes', as it was described by the famous Tudor herbalist John Gerard.
Left Peas were a staple ingredient in the medieval cottager's diet. **Above** Vervain was once considered an aphrodisiac.

The housewife's garden

One of the first books to offer advice to the cottager and small farmer was Thomas Tusser's *A Hundreth Good Pointes of Husbandrie* (1557). Tusser, himself a farmer, addresses his reader in simple verse in a sort of compendium of monthly duties. While the agricultural chores went to the farmer, his wife was responsible for tending the garden:

> In Marche, and in Aprill, from morning to night:
> in sowing and setting, good huswives delight.
> To have in their gardein, or some other plot:
> to trim up their house, and to furnish their pot.

The book is intentionally didactic and practical. Tusser recommends 'Seeds and Herbs for the Kitchen', 'Herbs and Roots for Sallads and Sauce' and 'Strewing Herbs of all sorts'. But he also lists 40 'Herbs, Branches, and Flowers, for Windows and Pots'. Here the housewife may have had the chance to express herself creatively, using flowers such as daffodils, hollyhocks, snapdragons and 'Roses of all sorts' to adorn her window-sill or doorway.

Right A high summer mix of herbs, wild flowers and vegetables in the Bayleaf garden at the Weald and Downland Living Museum in West Sussex.

The sixteenth-century country housewife's garden was bigger and more elaborate than the simple cottar's plot. It may even have had an element of simple design, with flowers not just in grown pots and by the cottage door, but in formal beds.

Working from Tusser's books and other sixteenth-century texts, the Weald and Downland Living Museum in West Sussex has recreated a tenant farmer's house and garden from this period. Between about 1550 and 1590 Bayleaf was leased to a carpenter and yeoman by the name of Thomas Wells. A yeoman was someone who farmed at least 100 acres (40.5ha); Bayleaf covered about 130 acres (52.6ha). Wells was clearly not a poor cottager, but he was still a tenant and would have worked hard for his living.

Bordered by hazel fencing, Bayleaf garden is laid out in beds with a predominance of vegetables – beans, peas, radishes, parsnips and leeks – but also salad leaves, herbs and 'edible weeds', such as fat hen and chickweed. Surrounding the garden are some pear trees and plantings of wild flowers. The historian Margaret Willes, describing Bayleaf in her excellent book *The Gardens of the British Working Class,* writes: 'The overall impression … is of green, with occasional flashes of colour, like wildflower meadows.' The garden's appeal is in its subtle, naturalistic nuances: there are no bold groupings of brightly coloured flowers or overt attempts at artistry. As we shall see, this was an effect which later gardeners, such as William Morris and William Robinson, would attempt to emulate.

Oreilles d'Ours.   Primula Auricula var.

Enter the florists

From the 1570s a new breed of gardener settled in England. Persecuted for their Protestant faith, French and Flemish Huguenots arrived from the Continent bringing with them not only outstanding artisan skills but pocketfuls of seeds and bulbs. These 'florists' appreciated flowers for their aesthetic qualities and started forming societies so they could show off their blooms, exchange plants and encourage the creation of new hybrids.

This was a far cry from the simple native flowers and herbs of our cottager and small farmer. But the florists' delight in growing plants for beauty alone slowly came to influence even the poorest gardener. Favourite florists' flowers, such as auriculas, pinks, hyacinths and tulips, would become prized cottage garden flowers. By the 1820s, garden writer John Claudius Loudon was reporting that 'a florists' society is established in almost every town and village in the northern districts'. The cultivation of delicate flowers had by this time become the pride and joy of many a worker. Different towns and regions had their favourites. In Sheffield it was the polyanthus and in Paisley it was laced pinks. Meanwhile, the miners of the Black Country favoured pansies. Other cottage gardeners focused their attentions on growing prize fruit and vegetables. The gooseberry, for instance, was adopted by growers in the industrial Midlands and the North.

Back in the seventeenth century, Hampshire-based agriculturist John Worlidge wrote that by the 1660s there was 'scarce a cottage in most of the southern parts of England, but hath its proportionate garden, so great a delight do most men take in it.' Gardening was no longer a necessity; it was on its way to becoming a national pastime. In his *Systema Horti-culturae* (1677), addressed to the 'the honest and plain Countryman', Worlidge devotes a whole chapter to flowers. 'There are many Flowers that either for scent or show are raised on the more ordinary Country Gardens, that several Florists have taken a great deal of pains and care exactly to describe.' He then goes on to record about 30 plants, in what constitutes an early listing of traditional cottage garden flowers, including foxgloves, sunflowers, nigella, marigolds, cornflowers, sweet rocket and scabious.

Opposite above *Primula auricula* (c.1820s), painted by the great flower artist Pierre-Joseph Redouté.
Opposite below This plate from *Twelve Months of Flowers* (1730) published by nurseryman Robert Furber shows favourite florists' flowers growing in March, including tulips, auriculas and narcissi.

Romantics and eccentrics

As we enter the eighteenth century, our story branches off into the gardens of writers and eccentrics, many of whom were inspired – either directly or indirectly – by the writings of the philosopher Jean-Jacques Rousseau. Rousseau believed that man was happiest surrounded by nature, living a simple life away from the corrupting influences of society. A new breed of romantic intellectuals, enchanted by the idea of escaping to the middle of nowhere, started setting up home in rustic abodes. In this new idealisation of the rural, the cottage came to epitomise a more innocent, honest and altogether better life.

An early example is provided by an extraordinary pair: the Ladies of Llangollen. Fleeing their stifling aristocratic homes in Ireland, and the threat of either marriage or the nunnery, Sarah Ponsonby and Eleanor Butler eloped to North Wales. In 1780 they moved to Plas Newydd, a large cottage with 4 acres (1.6ha) of land. Here they lived together for 50 years, slowly remodelling their house into a fantasy of mock-Gothic cottage orné (more on this subject later). Theirs was a leisurely life of gardening, walking, learning and sketching. On their rambles they would collect wild flowers for their garden. They grew their own fruit and vegetables, and ran a model dairy and poultry yard. But unlike real cottagers they had staff, including a gardener, two maids and a footman. They were, after all, ladies, and although they may have believed they were living the simple life, this had nothing in common with the hand-to-mouth lifestyle of their rural neighbours. (The Ladies did in fact eventually overspend and had to rely on the benevolence of Queen Charlotte, who granted them a pension.)

Right Dove Cottage in the Lake District. **Opposite** The native British foxglove, *Digitalis purpurea*.

Plas Newydd became infamous for its owners, who in later years wore black riding habits and men's top hats, and was celebrated for what it represented. Romantics such as Charles Lamb, Robert Southey and Sir Walter Scott flocked to see this delightful rural retreat. Another visitor, William Wordsworth, was even inspired to pen a poem about the pair.

At the time Wordsworth was enjoying a similar idyll in his native Lake District, guided by his principle of 'plain living and high thinking'. Dove Cottage, a traditional stone house near Grasmere, was his home together with his sister Dorothy (and latterly his wife and children) between 1799 and 1808. Brother and sister adored nature, that great Romantic inspirer, and when they were not writing or walking, they tended their hillside garden, affectionately referred to by William as a 'little domestic slip of a mountain'.

Dorothy and William filled their plot with native and wild flowers, such as foxgloves, columbines and buttercups. Like many cottagers before them, they obtained seeds and cuttings from neighbours, but – unlike their rural forbears – they were also happy to pay for shrubs from the local nurseryman. In her famous *Journal*, Dorothy records her homely Lakeside life, noting the flowers she gathers on her almost daily walks. She describes the vegetables she grows and her delight in her rural surroundings. Such was the charm of Dove Cottage, its whitewashed walls smothered in roses and honeysuckle, that it attracted the attention of passers-by. No doubt puffed with pride, Dorothy one day noticed: 'The ladies (evidently tourists) turned an eye of interest upon our little garden and cottage.'

Samuel Taylor Coleridge, Wordsworth's friend and collaborator, attempted a similar life when he and his young family moved to a cottage by the Quantock hills in 1797. He had dreamed of growing vegetables and keeping livestock, and here in rural Somerset he tried to do just that, though friends

commented on the proliferation of weeds in his garden. Today, the National Trust has recreated the garden with cottage plants and vegetables known to have been grown in Coleridge's time. As a nod to his careless attitude to weeding, ferns have been encouraged to grow in crevices, while wild flowers colonise the ground.

By the early nineteenth century, the idea of owning a cottage in the country had become so popular that Jane Austen, herself a genteel country girl, poked fun at the fashion. Robert Ferrars in *Sense and Sensibility* (1811) declares: 'I am exceedingly fond of a cottage. There is always so much comfort, so much elegance about them. And I protest, if I had any money to spare I should buy a little land and build one myself … I advise anybody who is going to build, to build a cottage.'

Picturesque fancies

Indeed, from the late eighteenth century quaint new cottages and gardens began to be created, inspired by the Picturesque ideals of William Gilpin and Sir Uvedale Price. Gilpin defined the Picturesque as 'that kind of beauty which would look well in a picture'. He extolled the qualities of contrast and irregularity. Uvedale Price, in his *Essay on the Picturesque* (1794) celebrated such attributes in rural homes: 'The characteristic beauties of a village are intricacy, variety and play of outline.'

But it was James Malton, in his *Essay on British Cottage Architecture* (1798), who pioneered the fashion for the cottage orné, as this new dwelling became known. In his book he describes the cottage as 'a small house in the country; of odd, irregular form ... the whole environed with smiling verdure; having a contented, cheerful, inviting aspect'. This 'verdure', he continued, could include 'fruit-trees, creeping ivy, honey suckles, jessamine, or indeed of flowers of any kind, attached to the dwelling'.

Soon the market became flooded with pattern books for cottages. Many of these designs did not see the light of day, but those that did and that remain standing today are wonderful architectural fancies. Blaise Hamlet near Bristol is a particularly good example. Designed by John Nash in 1811 this mini-village of nine cottages exhibits those qualities of variety and contrast – and most definitely oddness – so dear to the Picturesque movement. Thick hedges now surround the houses, while shrubs soften the edges, offering the desired 'verdure'.

Throughout the nineteenth century similar model villages, instigated by philanthropist landlords, were built across the country. At the same time, inspired by a new social conscience, landowners started repairing and updating their workers' homes. John Claudius Loudon did much to encourage them. In *The Manual of Cottage Gardening, Husbandry and Architecture* (1830), he argues that tending a plot and having a home to look after can benefit the cottager not just economically, but 'in every way render him a better member of society'.

Left One of the quirky cottages at Blaise Hamlet near Bristol.

A variegated picture

At the start of the Victorian era, the cottage garden was many things to many people. While some plots were badly neglected or rudimentary attempts at growing a few vegetables, others thrived under the care of a house-proud tenant. We glean a sense of this disparity from the literature of the time.

Writing in *Our Village* (1824–32), a series of sketches on life in the hamlet Three Mile Cross in Berkshire, Mary Russell Mitford describes her own cottage garden. Its walls are 'covered with hollyhocks, roses, honeysuckles, and a great apricot-tree … and the little garden behind full of common flowers, tulips, pinks, larkspurs, peonies, stocks and carnations, with an arbour of privet … where one … looks out over the gayest of all gay flower-beds.' However, not everywhere was as rosy. Thomas Hood offers another reality in his satirical poem, also called 'Our Village' (1833):

> Our village, that's to say, not Miss Mitford's village, but our village of
>   Bullock's Smithy …
> As for hollyhocks at the cottage doors, and honeysuckles and jasmines,
> you may go and whistle;
> But the tailor's front garden grows two cabbages, a dock, a ha'porth of
>   penny-royal, two dandelions, and a thistle.

The ideal cottage garden – the one that was such an inspiration to later generations – is evocatively described by George Eliot in *Scenes of Clerical Life* (1857): 'a charming paradisiacal mingling of all that was pleasant to the eye and good for food. The rich flower-border running along every walk, with its endless succession of spring flowers, anemones, auriculas, wall-flowers, sweet-williams, campanulas, snap-dragons, and tiger-lilies,

had taller beauties such as moss and Provence roses, varied with espalier apple trees; the crimson of a carnation was carried on in the lurking crimson of the neighbouring strawberry beds; you gathered a moss rose one moment and a bunch of currants the next; you were in delicious fluctuation between the scent of jasmine and the juice of gooseberries.'

You can see for yourself this blend of the useful and beautiful in the recreated gardens of two Victorian writers, Thomas Hardy and Beatrix Potter. Hardy, a country boy, was born in a cob-and-thatch cottage built by his great-grandfather on the edge of woods in the Dorset countryside. The small garden and orchard (see page 115) have been replanted in a style that Hardy may have known in his childhood; even the old privy remains. One can easily image the hens, geese and pig amongst the cabbages and cottage flowers.

Beatrix Potter moved away from London in her forties to seek solace and inspiration in the Lake District. Her garden at Hill Top (see page 124) – with its long narrow path edged with cottage flowers (including many of the ones listed by George Eliot), as well as shrubs and fruit bushes – offers a picture-perfect vision of the cottage garden.

Opposite Looking towards Hardy's Cottage from its fruit and vegetable garden. **Below** The front garden at Hill Top in the Lake District, dotted with foxgloves and verbascums.

Arts and Crafts ideals

The late eighteenth-century Romantic idealisation of the countryside was further heightened by the Arts and Crafts movement, whose most outspoken advocate was of course William Morris. He called for the eradication of cities and for England to become a 'garden, where nothing is wasted and nothing is spoilt'.

By the 1850s the Industrial Revolution had started to take its toll. Much of the rural population was being forced to move to towns and cities, where factories offered a new form of mechanised labour. Workers lived in crammed, unsanitary back-to-backs and there were no gardens to speak of.

It was in this context that the country cottage came to represent a paradise on Earth, in every way removed from all that was ugly, unhealthy and wrong with the world. William Morris himself created his own Eden – first at Red House on the outskirts of London, then at Kelmscott Manor in Oxfordshire. In both these homes, he designed gardens inspired by a love of native and climbing plants and a personal planting style: 'Flowers in masses are mighty strong colour, and if not used with a great deal of caution are very destructive to pleasure in gardening. On the whole, I think the best and safest plan is to mix up your flowers, and rather eschew great masses of colour.'

Morris and his Arts and Crafts contemporaries believed that a house should look as though it had grown out of its garden – in the same way that old cottages are so comfortably embedded in their surroundings. With Red House, which Morris co-designed with his friend and architect Philip Webb, the integration of house and garden was planned from the beginning. Webb's plans include the names of climbers – jasmine, rose, honeysuckle and passion flower – that would clothe the red-brick walls. When the house came to be built Morris made sure that the fewest apple trees were felled in the orchard on which it would sit. Near the house, borders were planted with cottage flowers such as roses, sunflowers, lilies and hollyhocks. Elsewhere, Morris was inspired by the medieval principle of small gardens enclosed with wattle fencing.

When Morris built Red House in 1860, he was at the vanguard of a new wave of artists, writers, reformers and gardeners who would turn to cottages and their gardens for inspiration. These men and women recorded and celebrated them; some even helped save them from dereliction. In the process, they created the modern myth of the cottage garden.

Opposite above Red House near London. **Below left** Morris's 'Trellis' wallpaper (1862).
Below right *The Long Walk at Kelmscott Manor, Oxfordshire* by Marie Spartali Stillman.

Artists of the cottage garden

During the 1860s a school of watercolourists started producing tranquil scenes of English rural life. Often the cottage formed the picturesque backdrop to the villagers' daily activities. Typical titles such as *Taking out the Washing*, *At the Garden Gate*, *Feeding the Geese* and *Gathering Lilac* evoke the homely content of these paintings, created by Helen Allingham, Myles Birket Foster and Arthur Claude Strachan among others.

It is tempting to see all these pictures as oversentimental, 'chocolate box' depictions with a very heavy dose of artistic licence. (A few did in fact appear on Cadbury's chocolate boxes.) The demands of the buying public did influence certain artists – particularly Strachan – to beautify what they saw. White geese waddle along paths; friendly cats wait by the cottage door; tame little birds enjoy being hand fed. It is a picture of peaceful contentment in the prettiest surroundings, exactly the paradise William Morris yearned for.

A few scenes, however, particularly some by Helen Allingham, suggest a more authentic eye. Cottages are not always neat and tidy: one's thatch is getting patchy, another's tiles have fallen from the roof. Climbers smother the building to such an extent that only the windows can be gleaned. Self-seeders appear amongst cracks in a dry-stone wall. Sunflowers and foxgloves peek over an unkempt hedge while wild flowers have been left to colonise its feet. Unlike

Left *A Garden at Hambledon, Surrey* by Helen Allingham. While the garden is well-tended and the children well-clothed, notice the state of the roof.

many of her contemporaries, Allingham worked outdoors, not in the studio, which may explain her somewhat more truthful depictions.

Her paintings – mostly of cottages in Sussex or Surrey – were reproduced in an evocative book, *The Cottage Homes of England* (1909). In his introduction, the author Stewart Dick writes: 'If you look at all the illustrations of this book you will not find one cottage, no matter how humble, that has not its little garden decked with flowers. In its small space it contains so much.' It certainly does. Every patch of earth has been rendered either beautiful or useful.

That Allingham was more authentic than her contemporaries is further proven by the photographs taken by her friend Gertrude Jekyll. Like Allingham, Jekyll recorded the villages of her local area. Her book, *Old West Surrey* (1904) is a key work of social history, featuring over 300 photographs, including many cottage gardens. Here are the roses, the everlasting sweet peas, asters, dahlias and Canterbury bells of Allingham's paintings. There are the climbers clothing every inch of wall. And there, standing by the door, is the housewife with her bright white apron and bonnet.

Left *At the Garden Gate,* another lovely depiction by Helen Allingham, with an impressive garland of nasturtiums around the door.

No more bedding

What did Gertrude Jekyll, the most successful garden designer of her time, want with humble cottage gardens? Both she and her friend William Robinson believed they had much to teach the 'educated' gardener. Contemporary garden design was dominated by brash bedding schemes, a growing passion for exotic plants and a tendency to over-manicure. To Jekyll, Robinson and indeed William Morris, this was an abomination. Morris did not hold back, writing in 1895: 'Many a good house … is marred by the vulgarity and stupidity of its garden, so that one is tormented by having to abstract in one's mind the building from the nightmare of horticulture which surrounds it.'

William Robinson, a hugely successful garden writer and publisher, as well as a gardener himself proclaimed: 'Among the things made by man nothing is prettier than an English cottage garden.' Like cottage gardeners, Robinson loved native flowers, spring bulbs, self-sown annuals, creepers and ramblers. He had 'no patience for bare soil' and wanted gardens to be abundant, varied and informal. He urged his readers to grow wild roses through trees and to rediscover native hedgerow plants.

In his most successful book, *The English Flower Garden* (1883), he sets out one of his guiding principles: 'We hold that the only true test of our efforts in planting and gardening is the picture. Do we frighten the artist away, or do we bring him to see a garden so free from ugly patterns and ugly colours that, seen in a beautiful light, it would be worth painting.' Just as lowly cottage gardens had inspired Allingham and others to paint, so Robinson – and Jekyll – called for the new 'designed' garden to appeal to the artist's eye. Allingham would go on to paint Jekyll's own garden at Munstead Wood in Surrey. Jekyll, who trained as an artist, described gardening as 'doing living pictures with land and trees and flowers'. Her great drifts of herbaceous planting – highly sophisticated versions of the rural gardens she so admired – are nothing but painterly.

Opposite The Main Border at Munstead Wood in Surrey. **Above** One of several views of the South Border at Munstead Wood painted by Helen Allingham.

Small is beautiful

The cottage garden style had many advantages, not least its adaptability. It would suit any size of garden and needn't cost the earth. At the dawn of the twentieth century, the idea that you could create a thing of beauty in a small garden was music to suburban gardeners' ears. The Victorian architect J. D. Sedding even argued that a small plot was a blessing: 'Let no one suppose that the beauty of a garden depends on its acreage, or on the amount of money spent upon it … In a small garden there is less fear of dissipated effort, more chance of making friends with its inmates, more time to spare to heighten the beauty of its effects.'

Cottage gardeners could enjoy floral abundance even within a confined space. From William Robinson's time onwards, more and more gardens were made with this concept in mind. Surprisingly, though, not all of them were small. 'Would it be misleading to call Hidcote a cottage garden on the most glorified scale?' ponders Vita Sackville-West, about one of the great gardens of the twentieth century. Vita was the owner of that other celebrated garden, Sissinghurst. She was a close friend of Major Lawrence Johnston, the creator of Hidcote. 'It resembles a cottage garden, or rather, a series of cottage gardens,' she continues, 'in so far as the plants grow in a jumble, flowering shrubs mingle with roses, herbaceous plants with bulbous subjects, climbers scrambling over hedges, seedlings coming up wherever they have chosen to show themselves.' At its heart, Hidcote is a series of small enclosures, or garden rooms, in which beds overflow with flowers. Evergreen hedges act as walls, and visual punctuation

marks come in the form of topiary, which Vita remarks 'is in the country tradition of smug broody hens, bumpy doves and coy peacocks'.

Vita created her own highly romantic garden through lavish planting set within garden rooms (what her husband Harold called 'a succession of privacies'). Echoing Vita's words, garden writer Anne Scott-James believed that Sissinghurst – developed between 1930 and 1962 – was 'the last cottage garden on a grand scale'. A grand scale indeed. The planting at both Hidcote and Sissinghurst is more elaborate than in any true cottage garden. Nor are the plants restricted to hardy, old-fashioned flowers. Both Vita and Lawrence Johnston were quite happy to mix native species with more exotic or rare specimens.

Opposite View of the neighbouring cottage from the Old Garden at Hidcote in Gloucestershire.
Right The Cottage Garden at Sissinghurst in Kent: a highly sophisticated interpretation of the style.

Creating the modern cottage garden

While Vita was creating Sissinghurst, an altogether more down-to-earth garden was being developed rural Somerset. Sensing that war might be on the way, in 1937 Margery Fish and her husband Walter bought a derelict manor house in the village of East Lambrook. Both worked in the Fleet Street newspaper world; this would be their weekend retreat and their escape if the bombs started to fall.

Like many other couples at the time, they designed their garden 'with the idea that we'd have to look after it ourselves'. What Margery Fish eventually created (Harold died in 1947) is a modern adaptation of the traditional cottage garden. Within its 2 acres (0.8ha) are small areas, each with its own feel, but unified by an informal style and a mix of small trees, shrubs, spring and summer bulbs, ground-cover plants, cottage flowers and lots of self-seeders. As well as opening her garden to the public, Margery recorded her experiences at East Lambrook through books and magazine articles. Her message was simple: anyone could create a beautiful, year-round garden.

Far left 'If in doubt, plant a geranium', was one of Margery Fish's mantras. **Left** *Penstemon* 'Margery Fish'. **Opposite** Plants spill onto paths and colonise paving at East Lambrook Manor in Somerset.

'Nowhere in the world is there anything quite like the English cottage garden,' she writes in *Cottage Garden Flowers* (1961). 'In every village and hamlet in the land there were these little gardens, always gay and never garish, and so obviously loved. There are not so many now, alas … but the flowers remain, flowers that have come to be known as "cottage flowers" because of their simple, steadfast qualities.' Thanks to her passion, Margery Fish saved many cottage flowers from extinction. Today, her legacy is uncontested. Both her books and her garden, which you can still visit (see page 160), are an inspiration to amateur and professional gardeners alike.

The 1980s saw a trend towards greater labour-saving devices for gardeners, such as hard- andscaping and ever more disease-resistant hybrids. Concerned about this new fashion, a group of enthusiasts formed the Cottage Garden Society in 1982. Their aim was to encourage the appreciation and creation of cottage gardens through talks, visits, seed swaps and plants sales. In 1995 the Society appointed BBC *Gardener's World* presenter Geoff Hamilton as its president. It was the perfect choice. Hamilton was famous for his practical and cost-saving approach and loved cottage gardens. He even presented a television series and wrote a book on the subject.

His words still ring true today: 'Most of us, wherever we work, whether we're in town or country, live in "cottages" – smallish houses with gardens which may be tiny but which still, albeit for different reasons, are an essential part of our lives. In a frenetic, stressful world, we need our "rural idyll" more than ever.'

Modern cottage gardens are created in the country, the suburbs, even in the heart of the city. The houses in which they sit don't necessarily have thatched roofs or a pretty view of the village green. But what they all have in common is an unpretentious beauty, created by an attentive, nature-loving gardener with whatever means he or she has available. 'It is with special pride that the cottager clings to his garden … It is his own, and his labour there is truly a labour of love', wrote Stewart Dick in 1909 in *The Cottage Homes of England*. Things have not changed in this respect.

Left A beautiful blend of flowers and vegetables at Rustling End Cottage in Hertfordshire. **Overleaf** A classic combination of old roses and native foxgloves.

CHAPTER 3

THE COTTAGE GARDEN STYLE

An absence of layout

Geoff Hamilton believed that what characterises a cottage garden is an absence of clear design. The gardens of our Victorian and earlier forefathers would have evolved over time, with no predetermined layout other than the size of the plot and the position of the cottage. Nowadays a certain amount of preplanning is no bad thing. It will save you both time and money, but the aim is always to create a garden that looks as though it has developed naturally.

Many cottages had small front gardens. Sometimes it was just a narrow strip of soil, just enough for a few easy-going flowers such as snapdragons, wallflowers or hollyhocks. The medieval housewife apparently grew hollyhocks by the walls of her house in a belief that they would combat rising damp.

If the front garden was more substantial, a simple path would divide it, offering – quite literally – a straightforward route from the outside world to the cottage door. 'Country front gardens are a perfect example of unpretentious simplicity that really works,' writes Geoff Hamilton. 'Nearly always a front path runs straight from the gate to the door, but that's no artistic design principle: it's very simply the shortest distance between two points.' (*Geoff Hamilton's Cottage Gardens*, 1995.) Practicality before artistry was the order of the day.

In general terms, the cottage garden followed the tradition of a flower garden at the front of the house and vegetable garden at the back. Herbs would generally have been grown near the kitchen door, where they were handy for picking. But there were endless variations – as many indeed as there are cottages – as can be witnessed in the watercolours of Allingham and her contemporaries.

Right Margery Fish's cottage garden at East Lambrook Manor in Somerset relies on abundant, natural-looking planting.

Any straight lines that did exist – created by paths, walls, borders, rows of vegetables, fences or gates – were softened by flowers, shrubs and climbers. There was rarely much space for a lawn of any great size, or for lots of paving or hard ground. In any small garden, soil is at a premium, so why waste it? Equally, bare patches of earth would have been anathema to the cottage gardener, as indeed they still are.

There would have been little room for large 'relaxing spaces', such as a patio with table and chairs. Instead, a simple bench, or maybe a rustic chair or two, tucked against a wall or in a nice little nook, or simply moved from inside the house on a sunny day, would have sufficed to create a quiet spot in which to sit. Christopher Lloyd, creator of Great Dixter in East Sussex, well understood the comfortable charms of these small spaces. 'The appeal of the cottage garden is in its friendly intimacy,' he observed in *The Cottage Garden* (1990). 'There are no empty spaces, no lawns, no vistas. Everything is near at hand and the good scents of flowers like roses, honeysuckle, lavender and mignonette are trapped.' Every surface, not just the ground, was used to good effect. Walls, fences and arches supported all manner of climbing plants, while walls were colonised by little plants such as houseleeks and ferns and, often, the ever-present, ever-encroaching ivy.

Like William Morris at Red House, the cottager would have respected his site and its history. The plot might feature an ancient fruit tree or two, an inheritance he would have willingly worked around, and no doubt been grateful for. An old shed or lean-to would have been repaired, rather than ripped out and replaced. This culture of thrift and reuse and a regard for nature and the past characterises all cottage gardens, both old and new. The best cottage gardens are richly personal spaces. Every plant and feature tells a story, and the layers of history usually stretch far beyond the present owner's occupancy.

Opposite Aquilegias, forget-me-nots, foxgloves and other easy-going plants happily co-exist in this cottage garden. **Above** *A Spring Garden* by Helen Allingham. Blossoming fruit trees rub shoulders with wallflowers, tulips, narcissi and vegetables.

A jumble of plants

Just as the garden's layout evolved over time, so too did the planting, in fact both went hand in hand. As William Robinson writes in *The English Flower Garden* (1883), 'the absence of a pretentious "plan" … lets the flowers tell their story to the heart.' This lack of strict aesthetic intention and unsophisticated beauty is one of the cottage garden's greatest charms.

Cottage gardeners acquired plants and seeds in the form of gifts from neighbours and friends. Many of them, like Dorothy Wordsworth at Dove Cottage, also collected native species from the surrounding countryside. And some were lucky to inherit a few special plants from the 'big house'. When the Victorian fashion for bedding took hold, for instance, huge quantities of herbaceous perennials were thrown onto the rubbish heaps of the upper and middle classes, leaving rich pickings for our cottagers, who were only too happy to replant them in their little plots.

The cottage garden was added to gradually, each new acquisition placed wherever there was a free spot. Taller specimens may have appeared at the front of the border, happily co-existing with their smaller cousins. Unlike the highly planned Victorian bedding schemes, in the cottage border there was never any need to follow a hierarchical approach to planting heights.

Self-seeders were encouraged and gently managed. After all, these were free additions to the garden and useful for filling gaps, either temporarily or long term. If the tall spikes of a mullein were to show up on the edge of a path, so be it. Such random outcroppings would add dynamic tension to the planting. They would also create unexpected juxtapositions, many of which might be more magical than any devised by the human mind. 'Mother nature has an uncanny way of self-sowing two colours together that no gardener would attempt,' Christopher Lloyd wisely observed. There is a beauty in such randomness, and in trusting nature to add its own sprinkling of magic.

Right A cheerful pairing of aquilegias and geums. **Opposite** Closely planted flowers is one of the key features of the cottage garden style.

The result was a floriferous profusion, with plants happily crammed together. Such tightly packed planting meant that flowers would prop each other up, without much need for artificial supports. It also helped reduce weeds and create a beneficial microclimate. 'A layer of humid air stays around the stems, helping to prevent them from flagging on hot days,' Christopher Lloyd explains. As we will see in the next chapter, cottage garden plants were usually hardy specimens. More often than not, they would have been able to look after themselves with little assistance, other than being divided every few years.

The emphasis, especially in the Victorian cottage garden, would have been – apart from bountiful produce – on flowers rather than foliage. Nowadays a more balanced approach is often favoured, where foliage plants can be used to add year-round interest or soften what could otherwise become an eye-popping and somewhat chaotic display of flowers.

Left No staking is required in this border at East Lambrook Manor, where lupins and phlomis take centre stage.

Pots and troughs

Colourful displays of flowers are of course a key part of the cottage garden, and perhaps no more so than when it comes to containers. Way back in the sixteenth century, Thomas Tusser was instructing housewives to plant 'Herbs, Branches, and Flowers, for Windows and Pots' partly, one assumes, to each embellish their little domain. Pots on window-sills, by porches and doorways, or grouped together against a wall or by a bench, were a simple way of adding a bit of show to a small area. Lilies, lavender, sweet Williams0- and marigolds amongst others were grown in pots. Some plants, such as lilies, would have been brought indoors for protection during the winter months.

Some 350 years later, Gertrude Jekyll describes how pots formed part of an abundant front garden in *Old West Surrey* (1904): 'There were hydrangeas, fuchsias, show and zonal geraniums, lilies, and begonias, for the main show; a pot or two of the graceful francoa, and half-hardy annuals cleverly grown in pots; a clematis in bloom, over the door, and for the protection of all, a framework, to which a light shelter could be fixed in case of very bad weather. It must have given pleasure to thousands of passers-by; to say nothing of the pride and delight that it must have been to its owner.'

Some of the Victorian florists were so obsessed with their precious blooms that they built special staged 'theatres' in which to show them off. This was especially the case with auriculas, which need fresh air, but don't like getting wet or being exposed to hot sun. They look particularly attractive planted in single pots, where you can really appreciate each individual flower, proudly perched on thick stems tucked in a whorl of thick green leaves. You may of course prefer more varied displays – and the choice is wide, ranging from traditional beauties such as pansies, tulips, geraniums and

Opposite A simple summer planting of geraniums and marigolds. **Left** This auricula theatre has been made from salvaged timber and tiles. Amongst the varieties on display are 'Bradford City', 'Connaught Court', 'Lord Seye and Sele', 'Sirius', 'Brownie', 'Shaun' and 'Merlin Stripe'.

fuchsias, to more subdued yet useful arrangements of herbs and salad plants.

The great thing about pots is that you can move them around at will, which allows for endless associations. Pots tightly grouped together can simulate the effects of the most beautiful border. And as Christopher Lloyd once wrote: 'Pots are great for experimenting with plants.' If you want to see just how thrilling pot displays can look, a visit to his garden at Great Dixter will not disappoint. Here you will see pots of bulbs, annuals, hardy and tender perennials combined to striking effect. Since Christo's death in 2006, his talented successor Fergus Garrett has been developing the garden, including its container displays, with great skill and panache. Like Hidcote, Great Dixter is a cottage garden on the grandest scale. There are intimate garden rooms, dense plantings of flowers, lots of self-seeders and, famously, topiary. It is far too artistic and adventurous to classify as a real cottage garden, but it is nonetheless inspired by many traditional cottage garden elements.

Even if you don't have any soil in your garden, you can create a mini cottage garden with containers, and you definitely don't have to aim for a 'Great Dixter' effect. A simply planted wooden crate or an old half-barrel – or just few terracotta pots grouped together – are enough to produce the desired effect. After all, the cottage garden is about simple beauty, not grand statements.

Left A collection of closely packed pots can be as beautiful as a planted border. **Above** A simple trough with just a few cottage flowers can easily create the right look.

Gates, walls and other features

The charm of a cottage garden is in part due to its 'fixed' features, such as the entrance gate, wall, fence or hedge, and paths. There is nothing contrived or elaborate about such elements. At their best, they are gently weathered, bearing the graceful patina of age. Most harmonise so well with the cottage and garden that they look as though they have always been there.

Our old cottagers would have used local materials, such as wood, stone, brick or wattle. Anything that was plentiful and therefore cheap would do. Stewart Dick in *The Cottage Homes of England* (1909), observes the regional differences found in cottage garden boundaries: 'The commonest, and perhaps the most beautiful, is the simple green hedge … Sometimes wooden fences are used, and these are of various sorts. In Berkshire, and also in Wiltshire, you may still see wattled fences, in the Cotswolds dry-stone walls, and in Devonshire stone walls covered with whitewash, while in Cheshire stone slabs placed on end are sometimes used, as in the north of Scotland.'

Never austere or stark, both the gate and door were comfortably welcoming, much like the cottage itself. The gate might, in rare cases, be topped with an arch decked in climbers such as roses, jasmine or honeysuckle. In Scotland, the tradition was for two rowan trees to grow intertwined and form a natural vault – a defence against witches and fairies who, it was believed, would never enter through an archway of rowan.

Both gate and boundary would blend naturally together. Traditional wicket gates
were very common, particularly when the boundary was a hedge or wooden fence.
In cottages with brick or stone walls, simple metal gates were also popular. While
wooden palings allowed you to grow flowers through them, walls could be colonised
with crevice-loving plants such as aubrieta and valerian. Paths too could be home to
a number of plants, the sweetest of which is perhaps *Erigeron karvinskianus*, which
will happily sow itself in all manner of nooks and crannies.

Opposite Rustic materials abound in this
Berkshire cottage, with its red brick and
flint walls, weathered blue gate and stone
path. **Above** Lavender weaves through the
simple picket fence while a closely clipped
evergreen frames the window.

Both gate and boundary would blend naturally together. Traditional wicket gates
were very common, particularly when the boundary was a hedge or wooden fence.
In cottages with brick or stone walls, simple metal gates were also popular. While
wooden palings allowed you to grow flowers through them, walls could be colonised
with crevice-loving plants such as aubrieta and valerian. Paths too could be home to
a number of plants, the sweetest of which is perhaps *Erigeron karvinskianus*, which
will happily sow itself in all manner of nooks and crannies.

In the past, a cottage path might be made of no more than beaten earth. As cottagers trampled to and from their house, they would have compacted the soil creating a natural alleyway. Nowadays, few of us would consider this option – which becomes a sea of mud in very wet weather – and the cheapest alternatives are gravel and concrete. Concrete may feel like the wrong material to use, but given time it will weather and soften. Old bricks and stone slabs are more expensive choices, but can look particularly attractive, especially when well suited to the material of the house.

If you are planning to add a path to your cottage garden, make sure it is wide enough to allow for edging plants to spread onto the hard surface. This is especially important in the front garden, where you sometimes need sufficient space to move larger objects in and out of your home. Secondary paths need not be so wide.

Smaller, less permanent fixtures – an arch, seat or bird bath – should also be simple and unpretentious. An arch can easily be fashioned from wooden poles. If you prefer metal, make sure the design is restrained. The same goes for benches and seats. It is worth remembering than in the traditional cottage garden a seat would probably have been no more than two short logs with a plank or stone slab placed across them.

Opposite above Brick paths are highly characterful and work beautifully with the billowing planting style of the cottage garden. Opposite below A robin enjoying the bird bath at Hill Top in Cumbria. Left The main path at Monk's House in East Sussex becomes much narrower in high summer.

Hedges and topiary

As we have seen, hedges were the most common garden boundary: living walls between lane and front garden, attractive to both the eye and wildlife. They acted as windbreaks too and as useful supports for other plants. Paintings by Helen Allingham depict all manner of plants peeking over healthy, chubby hedges: spiky delphiniums and foxgloves, cheerful sunflowers and frothy shrubs and small trees like lilacs and philadelphus.

The very oldest hedges were mixed: hawthorn, hazel, beech, privet, holly and wild roses amongst others. What probably started as a simple single-species hedge, usually hawthorn, would over many years have been colonised by other shrubs, creating a wildlife-friendly environment with year-round food and shelter for birds and insects.

For many cottagers, particularly in the Victorian era, the temptation to fashion a shrub into a topiarised shape was too strong to resist. Small-leaved evergreens, such as yew, box and *Lonicera nitida* (known as 'poor man's box'), were ideal for this purpose. Many cottages had at least one piece of topiary. Depending on the cottager's fancy, it could either be representational – birds, especially peacocks and hens, were very popular, so too were teapots and cats – or geometrical, such as a simple cone or spiral, or more elaborate chess piece. Those who were formally inclined might go for identical shapes either side of a gate, and thereby create natural gateposts. Some topiary was so impressive that it dwarfed the cottage building. Surely there could be no more visually arresting proof of the cottager's pride in his or her garden than this?

Opposite A huge topiary peacock stands proudly outside a cottage in the village of Horton in Worcestershire. Painting by the English watercolourist A. R. Quinton, 1912. **Above** A topiary arch frames the entrance to this cottage in Freshwater on the Isle of Wight. Painting by Helen Allingham.

Right Topiary and thatch combine in perfect geometric harmony at Alfriston Clergy House in East Sussex. **Overleaf** Cosmos are one of the easiest flowers to grow from seed.

CHAPTER 4

COTTAGE GARDEN FAVOURITES

Christopher Lloyd once observed: 'There are some kinds of plant about which one may say that they seem right in the cottage garden – whereas others, highly developed by the hybridisers, look completely out of place.' What makes a good cottage garden plant? Thankfully, it doesn't take an expert like Christo to pick them out from the crowd.

The first quality to look for is a certain 'naturalness'. The earliest cottage gardens were filled with wild plants, so you can't go far wrong by choosing a wild flower or one of its close cousins. You could, for instance, plant meadow cranesbill (*Geranium pratense*), but there are many cultivated varieties of hardy geranium to tempt you. Each one will look at home in the cottage garden. The same goes for many wild flowers: bellflowers, campions, mallows, poppies, snowdrops and many more.

Wild flowers have a simple, honest beauty that chimes with the old-fashioned feel of a cottage garden. This means that any flower or plant that looks unsophisticated will usually fit the bill – like single tulips or plants with daisy flowers, such as asters and echinaceas.

Second only to naturalness is sweetness and often both go hand in hand. Little bell-shaped flowers like those of lily of the valley and bluebells have an old-world, fairy-tale quaintness, and so do columbines, with their famous little bonnets. Narcissi, sweet peas, nigellas, honeysuckles and astrantias all come under this category.

Then there are the bold and colourful ones, like a child's drawing of a flower. Bright and cheerful, and without an ounce of pretence, dahlias, sunflowers, cosmos and zinnias are worth their weight in gold when it comes to injecting late summer fire into the garden.

Just as you think you have got to grips with what makes a traditional cottage garden flower, you realise that you are missing a key ingredient: that touch of the romantic, so cherished by those sentimental Victorians. This is where the roses, peonies, delphiniums, lilies and lilacs come in.

In keeping with the cottager's simple lifestyle, most cottage garden plants are fully hardy, even if some appear delicate. Herbaceous perennials and a few shrubs and trees form the bulk of the plot, with bulbs, annuals and biennials adding seasonal interest.

The following plants are my cottage garden favourites, my own seasonal stars and stalwarts. All of them are tough and easy-going and each one is – to me anyway – utterly charming. But don't just take my word for it. Christo advises that we should not feel 'too hide-bound in our notions of what a cottage gardener should grow'. Some of my choices may not be to your taste, and plants not traditionally considered 'cottagey' may have qualities that make you want to add them in your plot. That is just fine. The best gardens are all about self-expression and never about sticking to a rigid rule book.

Opposite *Lavatera olbia* 'Pink Frills'.
Above left Poppy flowers and seedheads are equally attractive.
Above centre Rudbeckias have wonderfully cheerful daisy flowers.
Above right Glorious rich, red cosmos.

Winter

Stripped bare of its spring and summer lushness, the winter garden is all about shapes and contours. Topiary and trees come to the fore, and although the garden appears to sleep, there is still lots to gladden the heart.

To many cottage gardeners, hellebores are the stars of the winter garden. You could be a purist and go for the white-flowered Christmas rose (*Helleborus niger*), but I find the Lenten rose (*H. orientalis*) even more appealing. Its many hybrids come in tempting shades – from white, buttercream, pink and green to purple and almost black. The downward-nodding, saucer-shaped flowers – either single or double, and sometimes freckled – look their best when seen through winter sunlight. All hellebores like humus-rich soil and a shady spot, where they will happily bloom from mid- or late winter to mid-spring.

Wordsworth's 'venturous harbinger of spring' is of course our favourite winter bulb: the snowdrop. The common snowdrop (*Galanthus nivalis*) would be my beginner's choice – easy to grow and extremely hardy – but there are a staggering 1,000 cultivars to choose from. All thrive in well-drained, humus-rich soil which is moist during the growing season. When dormant in the summer, snowdrops like dappled shade and are therefore happy growing under trees and shrubs. You don't need to plant lots: just a few bulbs here and there, as they will spread on their own.

Opposite Frosted stems add beauty to the winter garden.
Right Evergreen and permanent structures stand out in the snow.

Out of nowhere, on a sunny day in late January or February, the diminutive crocus bursts into bloom. Winter turns into spring; you could even be fooled into thinking it's summer. Bees in their tens and hundreds flock to its honey-scented flowers, their gentle buzz bringing visions of sun-soaked days to come. Winter crocuses come in creams and yellows, blues and purples, but my favourite is *Crocus tommasinianus*, which has delicate pale lilac flowers. Like the snowdrop it will naturalise easily.

Another tiny gem of the winter garden is *Cyclamen coum*. Its delicate shuttlecock flowers may look dainty but it's incredibly tough. It blooms from midwinter to early spring, in shades of pale pink to magenta, against a backdrop of plain green or patterned leaves. Like snowdrops, it likes partial shade and is ideal for growing under trees and shrubs. If happy in its spot, it too will spread.

Bucking the winter trend, a few shrubs come to glorious life in the colder months, like the heavenly *Viburnum × bodnantense* 'Dawn'. From early winter until early spring, its bare stems carry clusters of richly scented, candy-pink flowers. It's easy to grow and one of the longest flowering

Above Frosted flowers of *Viburnum* x *bodnantense* 'Dawn'. **Right** The magenta flowers of *Cyclamen coum* brighten the winter months.

*Above
Cotoneaster
lacteus* looking
splendid in the
frost. **Right** Who
can resist the
fresh whiteness
and purity of
snowdrops?

winter shrubs – an absolute must in my book. If you want a warm splash of colour, consider *Jasminum nudiflorum*. Its star-shaped, bright yellow flowers are also long-lasting, carried on long, slender stems whose leaves appear in early spring. Winter jasmine is quite a scrambling plant and is best grown against a wall as a 'shrubby climber'.

Of course, winter wouldn't be winter without berries. Hollies are the iconic berry-producing tree and very much at home in the cottage garden – but there are many alternatives, such as the semi-evergreen *Cotoneaster* 'Cornubia', which has elegant oval leaves and an attractive arching habit. Every winter during a particularly cold spell, my cotoneaster becomes a magnet for fieldfares and redwings who come to feast on the berries – a cheering sight indeed. For an even more bucolic look, the common hawthorn (*Crataegus monogyna*) makes a lovely tree or hedge, producing lots of bright red, oval berries known as haws.

Spring

Spring arrives and as the garden bursts into life many a gardener breathes a sigh of relief. The garden is now full of promise, with lush green growth and colour emerging everywhere.

No other flower seems quite so much at home in the spring cottage garden as the primrose (*Primula vulgaris*). 'But, tender blossom, why so pale?' Coleridge asks in his ode to this 'fragrant messenger of spring'. The flower's milky paleness is very much part of its charm and most welcome when it appears, sometimes as early as February. Its slightly later-flowering and brighter cousin, the cowslip (*Primula veris*), is just as sweet. Both are undemanding and will naturalise almost too readily.

Whether you like it or not, you will find it hard to keep the humble forget-me-not (*Myosotis sylvatica*) out of your garden. This biennial is a rampant self-seeder, but who wouldn't want a haze of baby-blue flowers gracing their plot? Blooming from April to June, forget-me-nots make great filler plants and are perfect companions to tulips and narcissi and many other spring flowers.

Another reliable spring favourite is the grape hyacinth (*Muscari armeniacum*). Its cone-shaped spikes of blue flowers appear in April and May. They love sunny, well-drained spots and look lovely in pots too.

Right Honesty and tulips amongst emerging perennials. **Opposite above** *Primula vulgaris*, our wild primrose. **Opposite below** Tulips and forget-me-nots: a classic combination.

Blues and yellows are mainstays of the spring colour wheel, a classic and winning combination that may even occur in your garden without you planning it (blame those forget-me-nots!). More blues – but also reds, pinks, purples and whites – can be enjoyed from the most easy-going of spring flowers: the pulmonarias. They are happy in any soil and will tolerate most conditions, although shade is their preferred location, perfect for those seemingly inhospitable nooks and crannies. The funnel-shaped flowers are small relative to the amount of foliage, but both are attractive. With some varieties the leaves are speckled with silver spots and blotches, useful for adding lightness in a dark corner. And bees absolutely adore them.

We've yet to mention Wordsworth's famous daffodils, the most cheerful of spring flowers. There are many types to choose from, but in my garden I stick to simple varieties rather than double or split-corona daffodils. I have a soft spot for the little pheasant's eye narcissus (*Narcissus poeticus* var. *recurvus*). One of the oldest cultivated daffs, it has the benefit of also being wonderfully scented. *Narcissus pseudonarcissus* is the native British daffodil, Wordsworth's inspirer and mood-lifter, also known as the Lent lily. Pale yellow with a slightly darker trumpet, it is robust and very long-flowering.

Above left The spring snowflake, *Leucojum vernum*. Above right Easy-going and reliable, the flowering currant is a great way to add a mass of spring colour to your garden. Opposite *Lamprocapnos spectabilis* 'Gold Heart'.

Closely related and often confused with the snowdrop, the spring snowflake (*Leucojum vernum*) is a wonderful bulb for a sunny spot. Delicate sprays of cup-shaped white flowers, each petal with a little green speck at its tip, appear between March and April. It likes moist, well-drained soil.

Whichever tulips you choose, they will always be at home in the cottage garden. For great masses of brilliant colour in late spring – in almost every conceivable shade – they are unsurpassed. If you want a modest, rustic look, stick with single-flowered varieties in shades of red, yellow, orange or pink. A few doubles, parrots and lily-flowered specimens may well creep in though, if like me, you cannot resist adding new varieties to your plot every year.

More spring plants

* Crown imperial (*Fritillaria imperialis*)
* Garden hyacinth (*Hyacinth orientalis*)
* Common lilac (*Syringa vulgaris*)
* Lily of the valley (*Convallaria majalis*)
* Siberian bugloss (*Brunnera macrophylla*)
* Spring vetchling (*Lathyrus vernus*)
* Wallflower (*Erysimum*)

There is one spring flower you should grow for its name only: bleeding heart (*Lamprocapnos spectabilis*). Graceful, arching sprays of heart-shaped pink flowers appear in late spring above attractive, fern-like leaves. It is very easy to grow, preferring a sheltered, sunny or part-shaded spot and humus-rich soil. Look out for paler pink, white and deep crimson varieties too.

Late spring into early summer is all about blossom and many cottage gardens have at least one apple, plum or cherry tree. If you don't have room for a tree in your garden, then a spring-flowering shrub is a good substitute. Rewarding and easy-going, the flowering currant (*Ribes sanguineum*) will tolerate all sorts of soil types and growing conditions and reward you with clusters of rosy-red tubular flowers from April. 'Pulborough Scarlet' is one of the best and prettiest of the red-flowering varieties.

Summer

Gardens often reach their peak of prettiness as the longest day approaches. The choice of summer plants is vast; it helps to think of them in the following categories, making sure you have a few of each.

BORDER FILLERS

These are the stalwarts of your summer garden: the doers and mixers, without which your borders wouldn't amount to much.

Early in the season, one of the most reliable plants are the hardy geraniums. Margery Fish (see page 160) famously advised: 'When in doubt, plant a geranium.' She was right, of course: there are geraniums for every situation, from moist shade to hot sun. Many are evergreen, making them brilliant ground-cover plants, and some have attractive autumn foliage, too.

The meadow cranesbill or geranium (*Geranium pratense*), a true wild flower, was a favourite in old cottage gardens. I particularly like its cultivated cousin, 'Mrs Kendall Clark' – a lighter lavender blue and incredibly easy-going. Other classic geraniums include the black-eyed, bright magenta *Geranium psilostemon*, which can reach 4ft (1.2m) and flowers into the autumn, and the small-flowered *G. phaeum*, also known as dusky cranesbill or black widow, because of its near-black flowers.

Opposite above *Geranium pratense* 'Mrs Kendall Clark'.
Opposite below *Linaria purpurea*, commonly known as toadflax.
Left Delphiniums, self-sown poppies and hardy geraniums in one of the borders at Alfriston Clergy House in East Sussex.

A very close second in my list of early summer must-haves are columbines. Your garden may already be populated with old-fashioned granny's bonnets (*Aquilegia vulgaris*), their dainty nodding flowers rising above fresh green foliage, often from late spring. Aquilegias are great filler plants and will self-seed profusely, in both sun and shade. Some varieties are a little gaudy, with over-large flowers and disappointing colours, but others are exquisite, such as *Aquilegia vulgaris* var. *stellata* 'Ruby Port' and *A*. 'Petticoat Pink'.

With its slender spires and tiny snapdragon flowers, the purple toadflax (*Linaria purpurea*) has to be one of the daintiest summer flowers. It appears in May or June and continues blooming into the autumn, preferring dry, well-drained spots such as walls, crevices, gravel drives and sunny borders. It will gently weave itself through other plants, but can also stand on its own, as the whole plant is a picture of slender grace.

Astrantias go by the quaint old country name of Hattie's pincushion. Each flowerhead consists of several flowers held together on tiny stalks, neatly contained within a star-shaped whorl of bracts. *Astrantia major* is the species plant in the family. Poetically known as melancholy gentleman, its blooms are a soft blend of pale green and white. There are also pinks (*A. major* var. *rosea*, *A*. 'Roma') and crimsons (*A. major* 'Ruby Wedding' and 'Hadspen Blood'). Astrantias are very soil-tolerant and will thrive in either full sun or part shade.

Bell-shaped flowers have a simple charm that gladdens the soul. Anne Brontë described bluebells as 'fairy gifts'. I think the same of campanulas: they are to summer what the bluebell is to spring. *Campanula persicifolia* is the purest of garden bellflowers, with single, lavender-blue bells borne on graceful, wand-like stems in June and July. Whenever I have a bare spot, I am tempted to fill it with this modest beauty. A taller, chunkier and altogether more showy variety is the gorgeous milky bellflower, *Campanula lactiflora* – a perfect back-of-the-border plant. Its pale blue flowers are held on broad panicles and look wonderful amongst roses and delphiniums. Both are unfussy plants and will self-seed freely.

More border fillers

* Avens (*Geum*)
* Catmint (*Nepeta*)
* Globe thistle (*Echinops*)
* Lady's mantle (*Alchemilla mollis*)
* Lavender (*Lavendula*)
* Ox-eye daisy (*Leucanthemum vulgare*)
* Penstemon
* Poppy (*Papaver*)
* Rose campion (*Lychnis coronaria*)
* Russian sage (*Perovskia atriplicifolia*)
* South American vervain (*Verbena bonariensis*)
* Yarrow (*Achillea*)

Right The pink and white *Astrantia* 'Buckland'.

Opposite *Campanula lactiflora* 'Prichard's Variety' amongst foxgloves, astrantias and geraniums.

SHOWSTOPPERS

Every flower border needs a few stars – stand-out beauties that draw the eye. In the showiness stakes, peonies come top in my book. The traditional cottage garden version is the deep red *Paeonia officinalis*, which actually blooms in late spring. The double-flowered *P.* × *festiva* 'Rosea Plena' is even more sumptuous. Other varieties, such as the *P. lactiflora* types, flower in June through to July. If you're looking to add some frou-frou romance to your garden, you can't get much lovelier than 'Sarah Bernhardt'. It has the biggest, blowsiest, pale pink blooms. There is a dark pink version, 'Karl Rosenfield', which is equally alluring. Peonies like full sun and take a year or two to become established. Once they have set root, do not disturb them: they will reward you with years, decades even, of knockout blooms.

Tall and stately, lupins are great statement plants. The spikes are formed of pea-like flowers and come in a fabulous range of colours, including yellows, pinks, reds, blues and purples. Some are bi-coloured, like *Lupinus* 'Gallery Blue', a mix of blue and purple. One of my favourites, 'Masterpiece', is purple flecked with orange. These duo-toned beauties can inject real vibrancy to a border. Lupins prefer a sunny spot and soil that isn't too rich, but otherwise are easy to grow. Make sure you remove the spikes after flowering to prevent them from setting seed, as this will weaken the plant.

Hollyhocks have long been favourites in the cottage garden. Come July, villages everywhere are embellished by their colourful nodding spires. They do best in light, well-drained soil and full sun: that's why they are so often seen lining cottage walls and paths. But they are also useful for adding strong vertical accents to borders. I prefer the single-flowered species hollyhocks (*Alcea rosea*), which can be pink, purple, red, yellow or cream. Once you have planted the seeds, there is a certain thrill in not knowing what colour your hollyhock will eventually be. Doubles – such as the aptly named Powder Puff Group – are a bit over the top, but semis, including 'Crème de Cassis', are charming, although harder to come by. When they

Opposite above *Paeonia lactiflora* 'Sarah Bernhardt'. **Opposite below** Delicate, duo-tone lupins. **Above** A mass of hollyhocks.

have found their happy spot, hollyhocks will self-seed with abandon. And this is just as well. Even though they are perennials, after two years or so they often succumb to a fungal disease known as rust. Their little replacements are there to save the day and perpetuate the summer flowering.

Foxgloves are perhaps the ultimate cottage flower, and with their tall spires of purple-pink bells common foxgloves (*Digitalis purpurea*) are the real deal. They are best grown in clumps and waves, as they appear in their natural woodland setting. The all-white variety (*D. purpurea* f. *albiflora*) is ideal for lighting up a dark corner, and there are lovely apricots too (*D. purpurea* 'Sutton's Apricot'). All foxgloves prefer part shade to full sun and like moist, rich soil. Most are biennial, which means they need to be planted in two consecutive years, so that new flowers appear every year. An exception is the shorter, butter-yellow *D. grandiflora*, a perennial, which looks great with blue and purple flowers.

Of course, a cottage garden wouldn't be worthy of its name without at least one rose, whether it be climbing, rambling or shrub. Old-fashioned and English roses are the ones to plant in the cottage border, avoiding at all costs the stiff and charmless Hybrid Teas. The more romantic looking, the better.

More showstoppers

* Daylily (*Hemerocallis*)
* *Delphinium*
* Mallow (*Malva*)
* Mullein (*Verbascum*)
* *Phlox*
* Red-hot poker (*Kniphofia*)
* Sword lily (*Gladiolus*)

Finally, a word about lilies. In small doses, these are a wonderful addition, adding a touch of romance and opulence. If I had to choose just one, it would be *Lilium regale*. The large, trumpet flowers are magnificent both in the border and in large containers – and they smell divine.

Left The spectacular and gloriously scented *Lilium regale*.
Above Dramatic spires of foxgloves and delphiniums.
Right *Rosa 'Madame Isaac Péreire'* amongst campanulas.

SUMMER ANNUALS

One of the great joys of gardening is growing a plant from seed. It's cheap, rewarding and often simpler than you think. Thrifty cottage gardeners have always swapped and saved seeds, ready for planting the following year. Here some of the easiest and prettiest annuals you can try.

One of the flowers most associated with the cottage garden is the sweet pea. If you want to add a mass of colour and scent to your garden, and indeed your house, all summer long, there is nothing better. The more you pick them, the more they flower. Grown up wigwams, sweet peas look good both in the flower border and the vegetable bed – and there is a rainbow of colours to choose from. I recommend you try – at least once – *Lathyrus odoratus* 'Cupani'. First introduced from Sicily in 1699, it is the oldest of all sweet peas and although its flowers are smaller than cultivated sweet peas, they have the most intense scent. A note on fragrance: some of the larger-flowered varieties do not smell, so check before you buy your seeds. All sweet peas like rich soil and can be planted *in situ*.

Do not confuse the annual sweet pea with its non-scented relative, *Lathyrus latifolius*, the everlasting sweet pea. This is another cottage favourite, and very useful too, as it returns year after year, is incredibly hardy and has pretty pink or white flowers.

I am on a mission to revive *Clarkia elegans* (also known as *C. unguiculata*). In recent decades, these lovely little ruffled flowers seem to have fallen out of fashion and yet they are super-easy and they flower continually from midsummer to early autumn. My grandmother used to grow them in her vegetable patch, from where they would be regularly cut and shown off in a vase in the kitchen. Clarkias have long stems making them brilliant for cutting, and their sweet, frilly blooms in soft shades of scarlet, salmon, pink and white are charming. Sow the seeds where they are to grow in early spring, thin out in stages when they start becoming overcrowded and you should enjoy flowers from July onwards.

Another slightly forgotten favourite is larkspur (*Consolida ajacis*), also known as the annual delphinium, which I think is so much more graceful than its larger and showier cousin. The thin spikes of spurred flowers may look delicate, but they will tolerate most soils and conditions. 'Misty Lavender', a smoky mauve, has a lovely vintage feel, while 'White' is one of the most ethereal of larkspurs, almost like a ghost of a flower.

Opposite above left *Nigella damascena*, also poetically known as love-in-a-mist.
Opposite above right Cosmos and strawflowers. **Opposite below left** A wigwam of sweet peas. **Opposite below right** *Clarkia elegans*, commonly known as garland flower.

Who can resist love-in-a-mist? Its evocative name is enough to make you want to plant it, but it is also a thing of exquisite beauty, like a finely crafted jewel. The flowers float amongst a cloud of feathery leaves and bracts, and when the blooms fade they are replaced with little puffed-up seed heads. *Nigella damascena* comes in shades of blue, mauve, pink and white, although to me the blues are its true colour. 'Oxford Blue' is a deep shade and the sweet 'Miss Jekyll' is sky blue. Nigellas like well-drained soil and are easily grown from seed, *in situ*. Deadhead regularly and you will extend the flowering into September.

Nasturtiums have been popular cottage garden plants ever since they were introduced from Peru in the late seventeenth century. Their bright trumpet flowers add a splash of colour to the vegetable patch, where they help protect beans, brassicas and other veg from insect attack. They do so by attracting aphids and cabbage white caterpillars, thereby keeping them away from your prized produce. You don't have to stick with the traditional bright oranges, reds and yellows. Unusual varieties include almost black (*Tropaeolum majus* 'Black Velvet'), peachy pink ('Ladybird Rose') or creamy yellow ('Whirlybird Cream'). Nasturtiums can be used as climbers or as ground fillers, occupying spaces when other plants have finished flowering. They prefer poor soil and will seed easily. The leaves and flowers are edible.

Right Larkspur, the wilder-looking, annual cousin of the delphinium. **Opposite** Blooming in late summer, nasturtiums are one of the easiest flowers to grow from seed.

More summer annuals
* Annual clary sage (*Salvia viridis*)
* Bishop's flower (*Ammi majus*)
* Cornflower (*Centaurea cyanus*)
* *Cosmos*
* Snapdragon (*Antirrhinum*)
* Spider flower (*Cleome*)
* Sunflower (*Helianthus*)
* Tobacco plant (*Nicotiana*)
* *Zinnia*

LATE SUMMER STUNNERS

By late summer the garden often reaches a colourful crescendo. Flowers in the hottest of hues fill the borders with a lively hurrah. Chief amongst them are the dahlias, which come in a dazzling array of flower shapes, colours and sizes. Some are so conspicuous they almost seem to shout for attention. Most gardeners love them for that – including Christopher Lloyd who claimed that their best quality was 'providing an oomph that no other flower can match'.

The singles, stars and collarettes are the dahlias to plant if you want to attract lots of bees and other pollinators. Cactus and decorative varieties are some of the showiest and the classic shapes most associated with the flower. Perhaps the sweetest are the lollipop-like pompom and ball dahlias. Whichever ones you grow, if you deadhead regularly you will have masses of flowers from midsummer to the first frosts.

Above *Crocosmia* 'Zeal Giant'.
Right Dahlias look great both in flower borders and amongst vegetables.
Opposite Dahlias and cosmos pack a floral punch.

Dahlias are very tolerant, but they do best in rich, free-draining soil and full sun. Follow instructions for planting tubers and make sure you don't overwater them before growth appears or you may cause them to rot. As soon as they start growing strongly, pinch out the tip of the main stem to encourage bushy growth. The plants need to be supported with strong stakes.

For a splash of fiery yellow, orange or red, crocosmias are hard to beat. They originate from South America, and in their native habitat the pretty, funnel-shaped flowers are a magnet for hummingbirds. Clump-forming perennials, with slender, arching stems and handsome, sword-like leaves, they are both easy going and vigorous. Used sparingly, they're a great way to inject a touch of exoticism into the late summer cottage garden.

Daisy flowers really come into their own in August and not just because of all those cheerful sunflowers. There are, for instance, the echinaceas. These large, attractive daisies have hit the gardening spotlight in the last 15 years or so, being popular in prairie planting schemes, but they have actually been grown in cottage gardens since the species (*Echinacea purpurea*) was introduced into England from the United States in the late seventeenth century.

Echinacea flowers are large and come in pinks, purples, coral, orange, salmon, white and green, all with a prominent central cone, hence their common name, coneflower. Most are single, some are double, others are frilly, and a few have slender reflexed petals. Echinaceas thrive in any fertile soil in full sun. Bees, butterflies and birds love them and they make great cut flowers too.

Rudbeckias – another daisy flower – come in warm shades of yellow and orange. Most have dark contrasting centres, which explains why the species *Rudbeckia fulgida* goes by the name of black-eyed Susan. Rudbeckias like a sunny position and relatively fertile soil. So too do heleniums, known as sneezeweed because they were used to make snuff. These sunny flowers offer yet more yellow, orange and bronze hues, and have pretty, jagged petals and large, rounded centres. I find the rich coppery-red shades especially attractive, like *H*. 'Moerheim Beauty', which looks particularly good with purple salvias. Young plants need protecting from slugs and snails.

More late summer stunners
* Bear's breeches (*Acanthus mollis*)
* North American ox-eye (*Heliopsis helianthoides*)
* *Salvia*
* Sea holly (*Eryngium*)
* Tree mallow (*Lavatera olbia*)
* Slender vervain (*Verbena rigida*)

Opposite Nothing beats a sunflower for late summer impact.
Above *Echinacea purpurea* also comes under the lovely name of hedgehog coneflower. **Right** *Helenium* 'Moerheim Beauty'.

Autumn

There is something magical about the autumn garden. The sun's lowering rays add enchantment and atmosphere, especially as they catch the burnished colours of turning leaves.

Michaelmas daisies really suit this soft, low light, which brings out their starry frothiness. And if you love lavenders, purples, pinks and blues, you are in for a treat. These are their predominant colours and the choice within these hues is wide. With their sweet little golden stamens, starworts – as they are also known – are one of the most floriferous and long-lasting of autumn flowers. Planted *en masse* they produce fluffy clouds of colour and are often accompanied by buzzing bees and a flutter of butterflies.

Right *Symphyotrichum* 'Ochtendgloren'. **Opposite** The soft October light beautifully sets off the turning vine leaves at The Courts Garden in Wiltshire.

Michaelmas daisies are so named because they flower around Michaelmas, 29 September, and although they are commonly known as asters, they have recently been classified as *Symphyotrichum*. With over 90 different species within this family, deciding which one to choose can feel a bit overwhelming. Some are tiny and clump forming, others are giants reaching 6½ft (2m) in height. One of the most popular and easily available is the medium-height *Aster frikartii* × 'Mönch'. With lavender-blue flowers it is one of the first Michaelmas daisies to bloom, sometimes as early as July.

All Michaelmas daisies prefer well-drained but moisture-retentive soil and a sunny site. Some varieties are prone to mildew, but New England asters (*Symphyotrichum novae-angliae*) are known for their resistance to it and need little staking, making them a good beginner's choice. You may, however, find it hard to resist *S. ericoides*, which produces airy sprays of tiny flowers. 'Pink Cloud' is particularly lovely; so too is the white-flowered 'Golden Spray'.

'It is sometimes difficult to establish,' Margery Fish wrote of the Japanese anemone, 'but when the plants settle down you have them for life.' And who wouldn't want them in their garden? Tall and long-flowering, *Anemone* × *hybrida* (previously known as *A. japonica*) is a picture of refined elegance. Its simple, often gently swaying flowers held on wiry stems produce a wonderfully ethereal effect.

Above *Aster* x *frikartii* 'Mönch'.
Right *Symphyotrichum ericoides*
'Pink Cloud'. **Opposite left** *Solidago*
'Goldenmosa'. **Opposite right** *Anemone*
hupehensis 'Hadspen Abundance'.

Japanese anemones prefer partial shade but will thrive in any soil and are also happy in the sun. The stunning white variety 'Honorine Jobert' is perfect for lighting up a shady spot. In my opinion they are all equally beautiful – whether light pink like 'September Charm' and 'Elegans' or a warmer shade such as 'Pretty Lady Susan' or, in the case of *A. hupehensis* 'Hadspen Abundance', a pink duo-tone. Once blooming is over, don't cut the flowers: the round, cottony seed heads look attractive in winter and are adored by goldfinches. Japanese anemones vary greatly in height, so check before you buy. The taller varieties make perfect back-of-the border plants.

Some consider it a weed, but I think goldenrod – with its frothy plumes of golden flowers – have a place in the autumn garden. The wilder varieties are indeed thugs, such as *Solidago gigantea* and *S. canadensis*, and are best avoided. If you want a tall goldenrod, try *S.* 'Goldenmosa', which has elegant sprays of tufted, mimosa-like flowerheads. Smaller options include 'Crown of Rays' (syn. 'Strahlenkrone') and 'Goldkind'. Goldenrods are super-easy, although they prefer full sun and well-drained soil. All are highly attractive to birds and butterflies.

More autumn plants

* Autumn crocus (*Colchicum*)
* Autumn cyclamen (*Cyclamen hederifolium*)
* *Chrysanthemum*
* Common heather (*Calluna vulgaris*)
* Hardy fuchsia (*Fuchsia magellanica*)
* Knotweed (*Persicaria*)
* Stonecrop (*Sedum*, recently renamed *Hylotelephium*)

Best shrubs and small trees

* Bay (*Laurus nobilis*)
* Box (*Buxus*)
* Butterfly bush (*Buddleja*)
* Fruit trees (including apple, crab apple, pear, plum, cherry)
* Hawthorn (*Crataegus*)
* Holly (*Ilex*)
* Lilac (*Syringa*)
* Mock orange (*Philadelphus*)
* Mountain ash or rowan (*Sorbus*)

Best plants for stone walls and crevices

* Basket-of-gold (*Aurinia saxatilis*)
* Fairy foxglove (*Erinus alpinus*)
* Ivy-leaved toadflax (*Cymbalaria muralis*)
* Mexican fleabane (*Erigeron karvinskianus*)
* Purple rock cress (*Aubrieta deltoidea*)
* Red valerian (*Centranthus ruber*)
* Rock campanula (*Campanula portenschlagiana*)
* Yellow corydalis (*Corydalis lutea*)

Right Japanese anemones in the September sun.

Best climbers

* *Clematis* (lots of varieties with different flowering seasons)
* Climbing and rambling roses
* Common white jasmine (*Jasminum officinale*)
* Grapevine (*Vitis vinifera*)
* Honeysuckle (*Lonicera periclymenum*)
* Hop (*Humulus lupulus*)
* Passion flower (*Passiflora caerulea*)
* Chinese Virginia creeper (*Parthenocissus henryana*)
* *Wisteria*

Best herbs

* Bee balm (*Monarda*)
* Borage (*Borago officinalis*)
* Chives (*Allium schoenoprasum*)
* Evening primrose (*Oenothera biennis*)
* Fennel (*Foeniculum vulgare*)
* Feverfew (*Tanacetum parthenium*)
* Hyssop (*Hyssopus officinalis*)
* Rosemary (*Rosmarinus officinalis*)

Overleaf East Lambrook Manor Gardens in Somerset, the twentieth-century creation of novice-turned-expert gardener Margery Fish.

CHAPTER 5

CLASSIC COTTAGE GARDENS

Anne Hathaway's Cottage
WARWICKSHIRE

Tourists flock to the pretty village of Shottery in Warwickshire to see where William Shakespeare's wife grew up. They snap away, lapping up this vision of cosy rural Englishness. It must be the most photographed cottage in the world. The garden itself has become something of a focal point, yet it has nothing to do with Shakespeare or Anne Hathaway. It was created by the extraordinary plantswoman Ellen Willmott in the 1920s.

The 500-year-old farmhouse was where the Hathaways, a well-to-do family of tenant farmers, resided. William lived a mile away in Stratford. Although no one knows how he and Anne met, there is no doubt that he visited her home on many occasions. When they married in 1582, Anne was 26, William just 18. A baby girl, Susanna, was born six months later.

In the late eighteenth century, the cottage became a place of pilgrimage for literary tourists. By the Victorian era it was attracting an even bigger audience. The cottage's last tenant, Mary Baker, herself a Hathaway descendant, was charging sixpence a tour and weaving stories about Anne and William's courtship. According to Mary, the young couple would sit by the hearth on a settle, which we now know dates from the 1700s!

In 1892 the cottage was acquired by the Shakespeare Birthplace Trust. Both cottage and garden were in a poor state of repair, but by the early twentieth century things were starting to look up. Photos and paintings of the time show borders filled with lilies, hollyhocks and delphiniums set off by shrubs and topiary.

Left This view takes in the vegetable plot on the left and the flower beds designed by Ellen Willmott beyond.

The garden's real turning point, however, came when Ellen Willmott (1858–1934) was asked to remodel it in the 1920s. Willmott was famous for her vast garden at Warley Place in Essex, now sadly lost, where she employed over 100 gardeners – all male, she didn't trust women in the garden – and cultivated over 100,000 plants. She spent her vast fortune on funding plant-hunting expeditions in China and the Middle East and developing not one but three gardens; the other two were in France and Italy. Willmott had already worked on the restoration of the garden at New Place, Shakespeare's house in Stratford, so she seemed the perfect choice for Anne Hathaway's Cottage.

The garden today is still very much in keeping with her design. At the front of the cottage are three large beds cut through by stone paths. Oak palings enclose the garden from the roadside, while box hedging and topiary near the house add evergreen structure. This simple layout forms the bulk of Willmott's plan. The three borders are currently undergoing restoration, one bed being tackled at a time, so visitors can still enjoy the garden.

The first bed has already been replanted and is packed full of herbaceous plants – so many in fact that at this point visitors slow down to study the flowers. In June it is a mass of roses, which Willmott especially adored, as well as pinks, violas, lychnis, foxtail lilies, achilleas, Jacob's ladder and lots of poppies. It is a densely planted, floriferous feast.

Right A wave of *Inula magnifica* is set off by a dash of electric-blue delphiniums.

Left A delicate climbing rose adds a touch of colour to the cottage walls. **Opposite left** *Potentilla nepalensis* 'Miss Willmott'. **Opposite right** *Ceratostigma willmottianum.*

The second border brims with tall perennials, some reaching over 6½ft (2m) in height. Elegant spires of veronicastrum, creamy froths of meadowsweet and giant scabious (*Cephalaria gigantea*) are followed later in the summer by a sea of yellow daisies (*Inula magnifica*) and Joe-Pye weed (*Eupatorium purpureum*), with its hazy clusters of purple-pink flowers.

The third bed is currently fallow but will soon by planted up with yet more herbaceous beauties. No doubt a few of these will be directly associated with Ellen Willmott herself, who gave her name to over 60 different plants. This seems wholly appropriate for a plantaholic who admitted: 'My plants and my gardens come before anything in life for me, and all my time is given up to working in one garden or another, and when it is too dark to see the plants themselves, I read or write about them.'

The most famous of Willmott's plants is the giant sea holly, *Eryngium giganteum* 'Miss Willmott's ghost'. The story goes that she liked to scatter the seeds in other people's plots. Two easy-to-spot Willmott plants in this garden are the stunning cobalt-blue Chinese plumbago (*Ceratostigma willmottianum*) and raspberry-pink *Potentilla nepalensis* 'Miss Willmott'.

The scene nearest the cottage is straight out of a Helen Allingham painting. Hollyhocks lean against the cottage walls before making way for climbing roses, underplanted with wallflowers, salvias and lavender, plus annuals for extra colour. The large sweeping box is still there, lining the path and providing a foreground to towering verbascums. Seating is provided by simple wooden benches, perfectly placed under the most divinely scented mock orange tree.

The rest of the front garden is made up of fruit and vegetable beds and a small herb garden. These were added in the 1990s and hark back to the more distant past, when the plot was predominantly productive. Only heritage varieties are grown and a few are particularly interesting, such as the oxheart carrot, whose large, heart-shaped roots are ideal for growing

in heavier soils. A bird scarer – made of potatoes and feathers, following a method recommended in a gardening book of 1858 – presides over the rows of fruit and vegetables.

Miss Willmott's ghost may not be present in this veg garden, but it is there in the lovely orchard, which she suggested should feature mown grass walks, wild flowers and spring bulbs. A wander through this peaceful spot is a pleasing counterpoint to the floral plenitude of the front garden.

Opposite left Tall spires of delphiniums in one of the Miss Willmott beds.
Opposite right The bijou herb garden.
Above Mown paths cut through the long grass on the orchard.

Oakhurst Cottage

SURREY

Oakhurst Cottage lies almost hidden from view, on the edge of woodland in a corner of the pretty Surrey village of Hambledon. It is a gem. As soon as you see it, you get the sense that time has stood still. And indeed it has. The last tenants left in 1981, having lived in the cottage for almost 40 years with no indoor toilet or bathroom. Their only modern convenience was a single electric socket. Thanks to its relatively unaltered state, the National Trust has been able to present it as an authentic cottage and garden from the early nineteenth century.

The building's origins are unclear, but they go back a long way. It probably started life as a barn in the sixteenth century. At a later, unknown date it was given dormer windows and first-floor access, first by means of a ladder, then via a rudimentary staircase, which you can still climb today.

This kind of small, timber-framed cottage would have been common throughout Surrey when Helen Allingham and Gertrude Jekyll, who lived a just few miles away, were studying rural buildings (see page 30). What is especially interesting is that we have an artistic record of the cottage, as Helen Allingham and her colleague Myles Birket Foster both depicted it. In Allingham's version, *A Cottage in Hambledon* (1888), hollyhocks and sunflowers poke their heads above a thick hedge, while unidentified climbing plants smother the front of the building and ivy clings to the back. Birket Foster's interpretation, *Gathering Lilac*, is a little more romantic. It shows a group of country girls picking lilac, while in the background the housewife is busy with chores, and geese feed in a distant field.

Right The garden in May is a picture of lush, emerging growth.

Opposite The cottage is bordered by thick woodland, making the garden quite shady, but volunteers have risen to the challenge, selecting plants that are tolerant of this environment. **Left** Self-seeded forget-me-nots add a sprinkling of powder-blue charm to the garden.

Today the garden is as it would have looked in the 1850s: only plants freely available to cottagers at that time are grown by the volunteer gardeners. The layout – rudimentary and undesigned as it is – follows a classic cottage garden pattern. A hedge surrounds the plot and is a traditional mix of hazel, oak, holly, privet, yew and hawthorn. Piercing it is a small wooden gate, from which a path runs straight to the cottage door, bisecting the front garden in two. One side is devoted to fruit and vegetables, with staple produce such as potatoes, onions, rhubarb, gooseberries and blackcurrants. A couple of bee skeps are tucked in a corner, protected by a small, tile-hung shelter. The other side brims with old-fashioned and wild flowers: hardy geraniums, pinks, red campion, foxgloves, hollyhocks, primroses and more.

Closest to the house and handy for picking are culinary and medical herbs: lavender, feverfew, rosemary, several kinds of mint, sage, tansy and bee-attracting comfrey. All herbs had their uses to the cottager. Comfrey, known as knitbone, was thought to heal fractured bones. Feverfew was used to soothe pain during childbirth and, as its name suggests, to lower temperatures. Lavender was used an antiseptic on stings and bites, and to help cure headaches together with many other ailments.

Among the mass of flowers, the narrow brick-and-stone path takes you to a simple wooden bench. Here the cottagers could have taken a few moments to rest their weary bones and enjoy the sight of forget-me-nots at their feet. From this vantage point, they may also have relished the beauty of a sculptural cardoon, with the added delight of knowing that its stems would soon be put to culinary use. Close to the front door, one flower stands out from all the rest. It is, of course, a rose. Given pride of place on a rustic arch, it serves no purpose other than to be beautiful and scent your path.

Opposite above Bee skeps are protected inside the small shelter on the right. Opposite below left A rose winds its way over the rustic arch. Opposite below right Solomon's seal lights up a shady spot with its white, bell-like flowers.

Around the side and back of the cottage, dark areas play host to hostas, vincas and hart's tongue ferns, some of which cling to the walls. Beyond would have been an orchard, though unfortunately this land no longer forms part of the plot. There is, however, a little area which the gardeners are currently developing with more flowers and herbs. Here you'll find the old earth closet used by the last tenants.

Oakhurst is the simplest, least pretentious cottage garden you are likely to visit. A modern-day cottage gardener could easily create a similar garden with a little resourcefulness and minimum expense. Everything is handmade, from the hazel wigwams and rose arbour to the bench, paths and skeps. The display of tools in the small barn to the side of the cottage bears testament to the manual labour involved not only in creating and tending the garden, but to the various cottage and agricultural crafts that may have been practised at Oakhurst.

All that is missing is a plume of smoke rising from the chimney, a line of washing in the front garden, and perhaps a few hens pecking at the ground – and you could be transported back in time. Oakhurst Cottage is a little pocket of history, of the not-so-distant past, and yet it harks back to a lifestyle that goes back centuries.

Right The fluffy lilac-purple flowers of meadow rue (*Thalictrum aquilegiifolium*) in the early morning light.

Hardy's Cottage
DORSET

Tucked away on the edge of woodland is a thatched cottage with a frothy foreground of flowers. To one side are neat rows of vegetables; a little further is a small orchard. Here, then, is our quintessential cottage garden: a charming blend of simple beauty and productive domesticity. Despite its remote location, this picture of quaintness has become iconic throughout Dorset, for it was the childhood home of novelist and poet Thomas Hardy (1840–1928).

Hardy was born and raised in this small thatch-and-cob cottage in the Dorset village of Higher Bockhampton. The surrounding area – its birds and trees, hills and heaths – shaped the young boy's vibrant imagination and eventually inspired his fictional Wessex, where many of his novels were set. Thomas had a strong affinity with nature. He respected it and was deeply inspired by it. Looking at his childhood environment, it is easy to see why. Just behind the cottage are Thorncombe Woods, an atmospheric patchwork of oak, sweet chestnut and beech teeming with birdlife. A little further away is an area of heather and gorse known Black Heath, where Dartmoor ponies roam free.

Opposite The front garden. **Right** A graceful jumble of ferns, everlasting sweet peas and roses.

The cottage was built by Thomas's great-grandfather, John Hardy, in about 1800. John was a self-employed mason with a small, yet thriving business. The garden would have been one of sustenance first and foremost, but to Thomas is was also a place of beauty. His earliest known poem, *Domicilium*, written when he was about 16, describes the cottage. Here are the first two stanzas:

It faces west, and round the back and sides
High beeches, bending, hang a veil of boughs,
And sweep against the roof. Wild honeysucks
Climb on the walls, and seem to sprout a wish
(If we may fancy wish of trees and plants)
To overtop the apple trees hard-by.

Red roses, lilacs, variegated box
Are there in plenty, and such hardy flowers
As flourish best untrained. Adjoining these
Are herbs and esculents; and farther still
A field; then cottages with trees, and last
The distant hills and sky.

Right Packed with roses and summer-flowering perennials, the front garden was originally created by Thomas Hardy and his friend Hermann Lea in 1912.

Above The fruit and vegetable beds, with rows of potatoes edged with chives in the foreground. **Opposite left** *Paeonia officinalis* 'Rosea Plena'. **Opposite right** Tightly clipped topiary is a feature of the garden.

Along with the 'honeysucks', lilacs, hardy flowers and herbs, the family grew fruit and vegetables, kept hens, bees and a pig, and had a small cider orchard. One story suggests that Hardy's mother paid for her son's education in honey. Another tells of the young Thomas giving the bookseller's son in Dorchester some apples in exchange for being allowed to read books.

Today the orchard is home to damsons, plums and many kinds of apples, both cider and culinary, including 'Beauty of Bath', 'Charles Ross' and 'Tom Putt'. Most hail from the West Country and date from the Victorian era. This historic authenticity is something which head gardener, Caps Browning-Smith, is keen to preserve. Whenever she adds a plant to the garden, she makes sure it is from the 1800s. The moss roses in the front garden, for instance, were adored by the Victorians, who loved their strange-looking, mossy sepals.

The vegetable garden is planted with traditional staple produce commonly grown by cottagers: heritage potatoes, broad beans and carrots, and raspberries too – including yellow ones 'because the birds don't go for them'. There is even a small nuttery, from which the hazel stems are harvested, just as they would have been in the old days, to make beanpoles and pea sticks. In another nod to nineteenth-century life, Caps likes to demonstrate the old-fashioned way of storing carrots, in what is known as a carrot clamp, where layers of carrots are covered in layers of straw and topped with a thick covering of soil.

In the early 1800s the garden would have been even more functional. Fruit and veg were grown in the area in front of the cottage, part of which probably also served as a builder's yard for the family business. The flower garden you see today is a creation of 1912, when the Hardy family moved out of the cottage and let it to writer Hermann Lea. Lea, who published *Thomas Hardy's Wessex* in 1913, was a close friend. Together they created the network of small beds, edging them with roofing tiles, no doubt found in the garden, and filling them with 'hardy flowers as flourish best untrained'. Here you will now find a pleasing mixture of moss and species roses and cottage favourites, such as hardy geraniums, lavender, catmint, lupins, daylilies and foxgloves.

Hardy's desire to preserve his cottage and garden is very much a continuation of the earlier work initiated by Gertrude Jekyll, William Morris and their Victorian contemporaries (see pages 29–33). In 1927, in a pamphlet entitled *The Preservation of Ancient Cottages*, Thomas Hardy wrote of the plight of old 'mudwall and thatch' cottages facing destruction from their landlords. He enjoined them to 'let as many as are left … remain where they are, and to repair them instead of replacing them with bricks, since, apart from their warmth and dryness, they have almost always great beauty and charm.'

Above Old crocks and tiles create the ideal habitat for a variety of wildlife, including slow-worms and lizards.
Opposite above Roses, geraniums and fading-yet-still-beautiful sweet rocket.
Opposite below Common foxgloves (*Digitalis purpurea*).

A visit inside the cottage, with its small rooms and low ceilings, its tiny bread oven and worn flagstones, gives yet more insight into the setting of Hardy's young life. His upstairs bedroom is where he wrote his early poems and novels. At the small desk overlooking the garden, one can easily imagine him writing the last stanza of *Domicilium*:

> Our house stood quite alone, and those tall firs
> And beeches were not planted. Snakes and efts
> Swarmed in the summer days, and nightly bats
> Would fly about our bedrooms. Heathcroppers
> Lived on the hills, and were our only friends;
> So wild it was when first we settled here.

Today the garden and adjoining woodland are still a haven for wildlife. Bats fly about at night and in spring the cottage's thatch turns into a giant roost. And there are slow-worms, adders and glow-worms. Hardy would be delighted to know that nature is still present in his cottage and garden, and that both are so lovingly looked after.

Left This mass of hardy geraniums has become the picturesque home for a pair of old watering cans.

Hill Top
CUMBRIA

'I wonder whether I shall do any sketching, or waste all my time gardening,' Beatrix Potter (1866–1943) wrote to a friend in 1906. The author and illustrator had just acquired Hill Top, a farmhouse in the pretty Lake District village of Near Sawrey. Her new garden did indeed prove a distraction, but it also became a source of inspiration and solace.

A few months earlier Beatrix's fiancé, the publisher Norman Warne, had died tragically young. Heartbroken, she threw herself into creating a comforting blanket of a house and garden. She filled the small rooms with old oak furniture and cherished heirlooms and turned the garden into a haven of peace and rustic beauty.

Inspired by its simple charms, Beatrix's first years at Hill Top were her most creative. The house and small garden, and the village itself, became backdrops for many of her well-loved characters. She delighted in recreating her surroundings and those who visit Hill Top today often feel it to be oddly familiar. Here is the long flower-edged path where the affronted Mrs Tabitha Twitchit led naughty Tom Kitten to the house. Here too is the little white gate and moss-covered stone wall on which Tom, Moppet and Mittens watched the Puddle-Ducks waddle past. And here in the vegetable garden is the rhubarb patch where Jemima tried to hide her eggs.

Within a year, Beatrix had planned and executed the layout of her half-acre (0.2ha) plot. Today it still reflects her higgledy-piggledy style of gardening and love of old-fashioned plants such as roses, honesty, hollyhocks and phlox. Much like Beatrix, the garden is utterly unpretentious. Fruit bushes and vegetables grow next to herbaceous perennials and shrubs in a pleasing blend of the practical and the beautiful.

Right The classic view of the garden at Hill Top, as experienced when you walk up the path towards the house.

When Beatrix bought Hill Top there was barely a garden to speak of – only a small kitchen garden opposite the front door and separated from the house by a farm track. To increase the garden space, she moved the track away from the house and added the now iconic slate path that leads to the house.

Her garden focused on four areas: the old kitchen garden, a large paddock, a small orchard and deep, long borders either side of the new path. Walls and edgings were made using local materials and at the back of the border adjoining the orchard, Beatrix added a long wooden trellis. By the summer of 1906 the beds were ready for planting. Neighbours were more than happy to help. 'I am inundated with offers of plants,' she wrote in September 1906. And when offers weren't forthcoming, she simply helped herself. 'I "stole" some honesty yesterday. It was put to be burnt in a heap of garden refuse! I have had something out of nearly every garden in the village.'

Even though she had a gardener, Beatrix was very hands-on. In her first years at Hill Top, she became 'absorbed in gardening' and did much of the planting herself. Over the years, the garden evolved as much by chance as by careful planning. She encouraged self-seeders, such as Welsh poppies, foxgloves and columbines, and let plants such as ferns and houseleeks appear in cracks in the walls. This was cottage gardening at its most liberated.

By 1930 she would claim that: 'My garden is a case of survival of the fitest [sic] – always very full of flowers and weeds, presently it will be a sheet of self-sown snowdrops, and later on daffodils. It always seems too wet or busy at the right time for digging over – consequently, I just let plants alone until they have to be divided.' Beatrix didn't shy away from physical labour, and when it got too hot, she would sometimes place a rhubarb leaf over her head as protection from the sun.

When the National Trust started restoring the garden in the 1980s, little remained of the original planting. Photos taken by Beatrix's father, her correspondence and the illustrations in her books were important sources of information for the team at Hill Top. Much like the garden's original creation, the restoration didn't follow a strict masterplan; it developed over time, making it all the more authentic, both in spirit and appearance.

For Pete Tasker, Hill Top's gardener for over 30 years, Rupert Potter's photos were crucial in understanding the range of plants grown by Beatrix. 'No plant is sourced that was not around in her time. Today about 90 per cent of the plants in the garden are historically accurate.' If you spot the occasional weed or untidy shrub, this is because Pete is staying true to the cottage style that Beatrix embraced.

Above and right The rustic, rose-clad trellis is underplanted with yellow lysimachias. **Opposite** A pretty duo: *Aquilegia vulgaris* and *Iris sibirica*.

The long beds are filled with a mix of cottage garden perennials. In spring, lady's mantle (*Alchemilla mollis*) reveals its apple-green leaves, while irises, columbines, forget-me-nots, hardy geraniums and honesty come into flower. In summer, yellow loosestrife, soapwort (*Saponaria officinalis*), meadowsweet, astilbes, acanthus, phlox and Shasta daisies (*Leucanthemum × superbum*) happily mingle with roses, gooseberries, beans and wigwams of sweet peas. Autumn brings a warm show of Michaelmas daisies, Japanese anemones, rose hips and pumpkins.

As with all true cottage gardens the house is clothed in climbers. Pale pink *Clematis* 'Elizabeth' is shortly followed by the sweetly scented *Wisteria sinensis* 'Alba'. A climbing rose with large deep pink blooms and pale blue *Clematis* 'Perle d'Azur' take over in during the summer months.

The little green gate opposite the house looks onto Beatrix's beloved vegetable garden. Here, despite the slight acid soil and the wet weather, four beds produce peas, potatoes, radishes, cabbages and lettuce, as well as raspberries, gooseberries and strawberries. A wooden beehive sits in the bee bole, exactly as it did in Beatrix's time, and tools are arranged among the vegetables in homage to Mr McGregor.

Looking out onto her Hill Top garden one February, Beatrix admired the snowdrops: 'There are thousands in front of the windows and in the orchard and in the lawn. This is why I have an untidy garden. I won't have the dear things dug up in summer, they are so much prettier growing in natural clumps, instead of being dried off and planted singly.' Perhaps it is in this unassuming little garden, charmingly tangled in places and left to its natural inclinations in others, that Beatrix's love of nature shines most brightly.

Opposite Lady's mantle (*Alchemilla mollis*) and native ferns happily grow against the slate wall that divides the front of the house from the vegetable garden.
Left Rows of potatoes and runner beans in the vegetable garden.

131

Alfriston Clergy House

EAST SUSSEX

Alfriston Clergy House exudes chocolate-box charm. What could be lovelier than a thatched half-timbered house on the edge of a village green, with church views and a riverside setting? But there's more: in the summer the garden is a picture of cottage sweetness.

Despite its small size, this fourteenth-century yeoman's house is highly significant, for it was the first property ever acquired by the newly formed National Trust. The fledgling organisation paid just £10 for the derelict building in 1896 but spent hundreds restoring it, under the direction of Arts and Crafts architect Alfred Powell.

Once habitable, the clergy house acquired tenants. The longest and most illustrious of these was Sir Robert Witt, art collector and expert, and co-founder of the Courtauld Institute of Art. He and his wife Mary used it as their weekend retreat from 1907 until the 1940s. In the early years of their tenancy the grounds were landscaped into terraces and garden 'rooms', and the plot transformed into a romantic and thoroughly Edwardian version of a cottage garden, complete with fashionable pergola, sunken garden, brick paving and topiary.

Left Hollyhocks and anemones by the entrance. **Opposite** Looking across the meadows towards the house and garden.

Above *Lythrum salicaria* edging the stream.
Right The deep magenta blooms of 'Rose de
Rescht' are the perfect counterpoint to the
wispy mass of golden solidago flowers.

When the National Trust opened the house to visitors in the late 1970s, the decision was made that it should look like 'a small private garden'. The main flowerbeds were to be inspired by the principles of William Robinson and Gertrude Jekyll. This remains the case, and head gardener Pete Keefe works hard to maintain the garden in that perfect state of tension between structural formality and planting profusion. It's a difficult balance to get right, particularly as the site is prone to flooding.

The garden sits on the edge of the River Cuckmere and every winter, part of it can be under water for as long as three months. 'Being chalky, the soil drains really well, so it's usually either water-logged or bone dry,' Pete explains. 'Trying to find plants that work with both is difficult.' For this reason, most of them are in now in raised beds, mulched yearly and fed regularly with organic fertilisers. This is container planting on a large scale.

The main flower borders face the river and are therefore at the mercy of rising water levels. Over the years, Pete has been able to fine-tune his planting, working out what copes with the conditions and what doesn't. It's been a case of survival of the fittest. Old-fashioned roses and hardy geraniums thrive here, as do asters, acanthus, achilleas and the old dyer's chamomile, *Anthemis tinctoria* 'E. C. Buxton'. Self-seeders find their way into the beds every year, often choosing just the right spot to complement their perennial cousins. There are dainty minglers like nigellas, feverfew and linarias, as well as exclamation marks in the form of opium poppies and evening primroses.

In June the terrace borders are dominated by soft pinks, blues and purples, enlivened by a few yellow flag irises. Most of the roses are old-fashioned, highly scented and once-flowering, such as the delicate-looking yet super-hardy 'Blush Damask'. One of Peter's favourites is 'Rose de Rescht': unlike the others it flowers throughout the summer, bearing an abundance of deep magenta double blooms.

Cutting through the two main herbaceous borders are steps rising to the house. Roses tumble either side of them, while a haze of daisy-flowered *Erigeron karvinskianus* further blurs your path. As if the scent of roses wasn't enough, you brush against the sweet, citrussy flowers of *Philadelphus* 'Lemoinei', and on reaching the house entrance you are rewarded with clouds of everlasting sweet peas. It's all so heady and wonderful, like a waking dream or an Edwardian summer.

Above The rambling rose 'Wedding Day' arches its way around one of the windows.
Right A cloud of old roses, including *Rosa* 'Blush Damask' and *R.* 'Celsiana'.

Above Hollyhocks and yellow daisies in one of the main borders. **Right** Monk's hood (*Aconitum napellus*) amongst roses.

Whichever way you decide to proceed, there are more treats in store. The pergola is draped in a white rambling rose (*Rosa multiflora*) and a purple grapevine (*Vitis vinifera* var. *atropurpurea*). It leads to the Box Garden, a quiet space marked by four 100-year-old box trees underplanted with fragrant cottage pinks (*Dianthus plumarius*): the ideal resting point after all that floral abundance.

Above Artichokes and fennel standing tall in the vegetable garden.

Opposite left Self-sown nasturtiums have popped up amongst the Swiss chard.

Opposite right The everlasting sweet pea (*Lathyrus grandiflorus*) makes up for its lack of scent with a mass of large flowers.

Nearby, the Sunk or Herb Garden is another formal area, but here the planting is more exuberant. Two small beds overflow with medicinal herbs known to medieval gardeners. 'These are not your traditional culinary herbs,' says Pete. 'Many would actually have been used by Edwardians as cottage garden plants and a lot of them can actually be found growing wild in the South Downs, such as ox-eye daisies, yarrow, marsh mallow and field scabious.'

By far the largest area is the vegetable garden – and what a beautiful spot it is. Within yet another formal layout, formed of eight rectangular raised beds, fruit, vegetables and a tamed wilderness of self-seeders happily co-exist. Towering globe artichokes dwarf all the other plants, adding drama to the scene. Below are rows of potatoes, beans, beetroot, chard and carrots, whose neatness is muddled by random outcrops of teasels, hardy geraniums, nigellas, poppies and nasturtiums. Amongst the wild flowers are a few cultivated beauties: a bed of gladioli and a handful of sweet pea wigwams, made from specially sourced Sussex-cut hazel. Look down for Corsican mint growing in the cracks in the paving; its strong aroma is known to repel certain insects and help protect brassicas such as cabbage and cauliflower.

No classic cottage garden would be worthy of its name without a few fruit trees. At the opposite end of the garden is a small orchard, where apple trees grow alongside the traditional medlar and mulberry. In early spring the meadow grass is awash with daffodils, shortly followed by snake's head fritillaries, and then buttercups. Amongst the apple trees are local varieties such as 'Alfriston', raised in nearby Uckfield in the late eighteenth century; 'Sussex Duck's Bill', an ancient dual-purpose apple dating from the 1600s; and 'Crawley Beauty', first recorded in a Sussex garden in the early 1900s. Like the terrace flower borders, the orchard usually floods in winter, so the trees are staked to stop them from collapsing when the roots start to rot.

Thanks both to its location and abundant planting, the garden is full of wildlife, from birds and bats to butterflies and bees. If you're lucky you might spot a kingfisher or a chalkhill blue butterfly, or see the 'resident' fox as he makes his daily appearance. On my visit a squirrel sat briefly on the roofline, his distinctive arched back and curved tail silhouetted against the sky. It was like an illustration from a child's picture book. Sights like these make a lasting impression and Alfriston lingers in the mind long after one has left. It's all so pleasing, so pretty and, for the cottage gardener, so inspiring.

Right The view of the church from the orchard, home to local apple varieties.

Monk's House

EAST SUSSEX

Virginia Woolf (1882–1941) and her husband Leonard (1880–1969) both adored the East Sussex countryside, its chalk cliffs, undulating hills and big skies. In their late thirties they were able to acquire their own patch of the South Downs: Monk's House, a small, weatherboarded building discreetly located at the end of a lane in the village of Rodmell. This would become their rural retreat, away from the bustle of London. Here they would read, write and listen to music, happily ensconced in the comfort of its small rooms. But what first drew them to Monk's House was not the building but its garden. The couple had already glimpsed it on their many walks through Rodmell and were enraptured when it became theirs. Announcing the news of their purchase to a friend in 1919, Virginia wrote: 'The point of it is the garden … This is going to be the pride of our hearts; I warn you.' She was right.

As soon as he moved in, Leonard became obsessed by his three-quarters of an acre (0.3ha) plot. He designed it, planted it and kept adding to it for the rest of his life. Virginia enjoyed assisting him. Like walking, which she loved, gardening was the ideal counterpoint to hours spent writing. She was never a garden designer or plantswoman, but she liked the physical labour – and no doubt the release of tension – that gardening afforded. One day she recalled 'weeding all day to finish the beds in a queer sort of enthusiasm which made me say this is happiness'.

Left When Leonard Woolf started designing his new garden, he retained some of the old walls, which have acted as graceful supports for climbers ever since.

143

Throughout her adult life, Virginia Woolf suffered bouts of debilitating depression. Her small country house, with its gently enveloping garden, was her refuge, far enough away from London's chaotic social life to restore her frayed nerves. Here she experienced 'snatches of divine loneliness' and here too, in her writing studio in the garden, she wrote many of her bestselling books, such as *Mrs Dalloway* (1925), *Orlando* (1928) and *The Waves* (1931).

The early years at Monk's House were anything but luxurious. When the couple moved in, there was no running water, bathroom or indoor toilet. They quickly discovered that whenever it rained the kitchen flooded. But as Virginia and Leonard started earning more money, the house was gradually modernised and improved, and life became more comfortable. Always, however, what pleased Virginia most about her home was its 'ramshackle informality' – both inside and out. In its all-pervading untidiness and charming rusticity, Monk's House was never anything but cottagey.

As early as 1920, just a year after moving in, Leonard was planning flowerbeds and, according to Virginia, 'entirely remaking the garden'. The plot they inherited had a few crumbling buildings. These were taken down, although Leonard kept the wall of an old granary which, along with established trees, provided the ideal backdrop for foxgloves, wisteria, roses and clematis. He recycled cobbles and millstones, found in the garden, and incorporated them into paths and paving, many of which he laid by hand. The previous owners, the Glazebrooks, had owned the mill in the village during the nineteenth century; Leonard loved the fact that he was including these relics of history into his new garden.

Opposite Taken from the balcony of Leonard's attic study, this view shows the dense planting of the flower garden with Virginia's writing lodge nestling in the distance.

Right The house barely has a front garden; its horticultural riches are hidden from sight and come as a delightful surprise.

Above Bright yellow lysimachias with soft purple *Salvia* x *sylvestris* 'Mainacht'. **Right** Pinks and lavender-blues: catmint, penstemon, cosmos and *Verbena bonariensis*.

He divided the garden into a series of small spaces, each with its own feel, but guided by the same spirit. Leonard was fond of bright, exotic colours, perhaps because he had lived in Ceylon in his twenties. His favourite flowers – zinnias, dahlias, kniphofias and roses – offered him a palette of strong hues with which to paint. But, ever the plantsman, he also liked white flowers, such as lilies and Japanese anemones, and understated beauties, such as hellebores.

Above A wigwam of sweet peas set against the cheerful trumpet blooms of daylilies. **Right** Dahlias and cosmos are a highlight in late summer.

There is a delicacy in the planting at Monk's House, partly because Leonard rarely planted in large clumps. He acquired flowers for their individual qualities and placed them one next to another, creating at times subtle, and at times electric combinations.

In the height of summer, the borders overflow with blooms and foliage. 'Our garden is a perfect variegated chintz: asters, zinnias, geums, nasturtiums & so on: all bright, cut from coloured papers, stiff, upstanding as flowers should be,' wrote Virginia. The garden cast a spell on her; its beauty stimulating lyrical descriptions. Still today, the informal, often dense planting coupled with structural divisions and focal points offer ample opportunities to pause and contemplate. This is fitting for the garden of two great thinkers.

Despite its visual appeal, there was another point to the garden: the production of fruit and vegetables. The orchard yielded huge crops of plums, apples and pears, while the kitchen garden offered up a surplus of potatoes, cabbages, parsnips, carrots and onions, which Leonard sold at the Lewes Women's Institute market. Here too Virginia played her part, picking and bottling fruit, as well as collecting honey from Leonard's beehives.

Right The vegetable garden, with its uninterrupted view of the village church.

Above The orchard in bloom. One of Virginia's favourite parts of the garden, it probably inspired her short story, 'In the Orchard'.

Leonard and Virginia were not working-class cottagers, but in their own way they resembled them. Writing was their cottage industry. They worked from home and were self-employed, relying on their labour to earn a living. Monk's House was not a place to come back to after a day at the office; it was the setting for their working life. Virginia was surrounded by the garden as she wrote in her lodge near the orchard, while Leonard kept watch over his flower borders and kitchen garden from his top-floor study.

Despite Virginia's tragic and untimely death, she enjoyed snatches of contentment at Monk's House. And part of this was due to the garden – what it offered in the way of beauty and physical activity but also what it brought to her mind. She once asked: 'What do you think is probably the happiest moment in one's whole life?' And, answering the question herself, wrote: 'I think it's the moment when one is walking in one's garden, perhaps picking a few dead flowers, and then suddenly one thinks: My husband lives in that house – and he loves me.'

Right The evening sun casting its warm golden light on the summer garden.

Plas yn Rhiw
GWYNEDD

Plas yn Rhiw is a cottage garden with a difference. It isn't set in a cosy village location overlooking the green or nearby fields. Instead, it is located at the very tip of 'Snowdon's arm', in the wild and windswept Llŷn Peninsula. And yet, in its own way, it is as homely as a land-locked Surrey garden.

'To those sailing bleakly across Hell's Mouth, there is just one spot where the eye gratefully rests on relative snugness,' wrote the architect Sir Clough Williams-Ellis. This favoured place was Plas yn Rhiw. Set halfway down a hillside and facing south-east, its small manor house and garden lie in sheltered seclusion, protected from the strong south-westerlies by the ragged tor of Mynydd y Graig.

That a garden should even exist here is down to the determination of three indomitable sisters – Eileen, Lorna and Honora Keating – who acquired the house in 1939. They were passionate conservationists and devoted the last decades of their lives to protecting the area, waging campaigns against commercial forestry, caravan parks and proposals for the construction of a nuclear power station. Like Beatrix Potter in the Lake District, they developed a productive partnership with the National Trust, acquiring land for the sole purpose of donating it to the charity. In their garden, they displayed

Left The network of low box hedging in the front garden.
Right Comfrey growing amongst the ferns and red campions.

Right An evergreen structure of shrubs and topiary ensures the garden has appeal even in the depths of winter. Opposite left Lovers of damp, shady and rocky places, Welsh poppies have made themselves at home amongst the cracks and crevices in the garden. Opposite right Moss and ferns have been left to smother the small wall adjoining the weathered steps, creating a magical, otherwordly feel.

this same respect for nature and the environment. Never overly controlling, their attitude was one of working with their site rather than against it. Still today it is gardened in a way that embraces this philosophy.

When the Keatings acquired Plas yn Rhiw, brambles had taken over the house; you had to climb through a side window to get into it. With the help of Williams-Ellis, who was concurrently creating the famous village of Portmeirion in North Wales, within a year the house was made habitable.

Honora, the youngest of the sisters, was the driving force behind the garden's restoration. What a delight it must have been to discover, under the brambles, bracken and weeds, a network of box-lined paths and the remains of a box parterre in front of the house. This was reinstated and a few judiciously placed topiarised yews and boxes were also added to the garden.

Within this formal structure, nature was left relatively untamed. Along the paved and cobbled paths, hardy geraniums, Welsh poppies and ferns grew wherever they could, while moss and lichen clothed the garden in a veil of timeless beauty. Old walls dripped with ivy-leaved toadflax. Crevices and banks were colonised by wild primroses, hart's tongue fern and lady's mantle (*Alchemilla mollis*).

With its narrow pathways, its twists and turns and small compartments, it would be easy to think of this small 1-acre (0.4ha) garden as inward looking. Yet your eye is constantly being pulled towards the magnificent views of the sea beyond, in a delicious to-and-fro that offers the perfect balance of comforting intimacy and sublime grandeur.

Left The vista from the top terrace offer views of the box parterre and glimpses of the sea.

Today, native wild flowers, such as foxgloves, aquilegias and red campion, together with hardy cottage garden plants and shrubs of sweet bay and cherry laurel, happily coexist with a sprinkling of exotic beauties. Honora Keating was a keen plantswoman and could not resist adding a few tender plants to her garden, such as *Abutilon* 'Ashford Red', which flowers almost continuously in the shelter of the veranda.

The box parterre in front of the house, recently replanted by Head Gardener Llifon Jones, is a hard-working blend of repeat-flowering shrub roses, perennials, bulbs, annuals and biennials in shades of pink, white, blue and purple. Amongst the roses are the popular David Austin varieties 'Harlow Carr' and 'Eglantyne' and 'The Mayflower'. The hardy cottage favourites – including phlox, lupins, hardy geraniums, Japanese anemones and echinaceas – are further enhanced by annuals, not least the wonderfully long-flowering and scented tobacco plants (*Nicotiana mutabilis* 'Marshmallow' and *N.* × *hybrida* 'Whisper Mixed') and the ever-reliable *Cosmos bipinnatus* 'Purity'.

In keeping with the sisters' love of nature the garden is managed organically. In fact, Plas yn Rhiw is currently the only organic National Trust garden in Wales. Now, as it was in their day, it is both beautiful and productive. The small vegetable garden has been reinstated and, above the house, a new orchard, filled with native Welsh fruit trees and a mass of wild flowers in spring, is maturing.

Above A wooden fence acts as a rustic enclosure at the back of the cottage. **Opposite** A mass of red campion, a pretty wild flower commonly found in woodlands and on roadside verges.

East Lambrook Manor
SOMERSET

Margery Fish (1892–1969) is an inspiring figure. She started gardening in her mid-forties and without any training created a plant-packed paradise that has redefined the cottage garden style. Her ideas, and the garden in which she practised them, have become so influential that she has been dubbed 'the mother of modern gardening'.

Whereas Gertrude Jekyll took inspiration from cottage gardens to create large, showy borders, Margery Fish's approach was on a domestic and achievable scale. Hers was a practical, modern-day reinterpretation for the contemporary gardener, with added ingredients. Ground-cover plants were encouraged, both to help suppress weeds and create a backdrop for flowers. She thought a garden could look good all year round and that it could be maintained without the assistance of a paid gardener. This was music to the ears of the gardening public – and so was her candour.

'Of course we made mistakes, endless mistakes, but at least they were our own, just as the garden was our own. However imperfect the result there is a certain satisfaction in making a garden that is like no one else's,' writes Margery Fish in the introduction to her first book, *We Made a Garden* (1956). She went on to pen another seven gardening books and hundreds of articles. Her fresh approach made people feel it was alright to give it a go and that, as in all true cottage gardens, self-expression was all-important.

Right Dawn rises over East Lambrook Manor's exquisite silver garden.

Above Looking towards the old manor house, which is tucked away in a corner of the garden. **Opposite left** Even the most unassuming corner has its charm in this abundant garden, where plants are encouraged to set seed and fill the space. **Opposite right** Narrow paths twist and turn.

Margery and her husband Walter came from the Fleet Street newspaper world, where they had enjoyed long careers. He had been editor-in-chief of the *Daily Mail* and she his personal secretary for many years. In 1937, sensing the threat of war, Walter decided to buy a house in the country. Their London friends showed concern when the couple acquired a 'poor battered old house … and a wilderness of a garden' in deepest Somerset. But, as Margery confessed: 'I never regretted our foolhardiness.' This was her chance to create a garden 'as modest and unpretentious as the house, a cottage garden in fact, with crooked paths and unexpected corners'.

The development of the garden was not without its own unexpected turns, some of which stemmed from the couple's opposing views. Walter loved big showy flowers such as dahlias; Margery loved small, delicate beauties like primulas. He liked neat paths and paving free of plants; she liked nothing more than self-seeders appearing in cracks and crevices.

Despite their clashes, both agreed that the garden should have 'a good bone structure'. Hard landscaping in the form of raised beds, paths and terraces, but also evergreens and trees, made up the skeleton of the garden. But unlike Sissinghurst or Hidcote, the garden is not a series of rooms. It is made up of linked areas and, despite being under 2 acres (0.8ha), packs in a huge amount, both in terms of variety of conditions and planting and in terms of individual plants.

The house itself – an old manor of warm honey-coloured stone known as hamstone – is tucked away in a corner of the garden. A much more dominant feature is the large seventeenth-century Malthouse, now a café and art gallery, which sits in the centre of the garden. Its position helps define a natural circuit, as the garden wraps itself around it.

The Terrace, on rising ground beside the house, is where the Margery and Walter started developing the garden and, fittingly, where most visitors start their journey. A line of clipped *Chamaecyparis lawsoniana* 'Fletcheri', or 'pudding trees' as Margaret Fish called them, cuts across this spot. Here is our first sight of what Margery called 'the intelligent use of evergreen plants'. Such formal touches helped add a sense of order and repose to her busy, mingled planting.

On the Terrace's sloping site, Margery and Water gave themselves a tough challenge. Between a series of narrow stone paths, they added island beds. These would have to look good from all angles and be designed to work together, as one inevitably acted as a backdrop to another. The planting in the beds is particularly dense and it can take time for your eye to adjust to the floral profusion. In May it is a jumble of aquilegias, geums, Welsh poppies, forget-me-nots, irises, hardy geraniums, salvias, wallflowers, and emerging lupins and foxgloves. And there are shrubs too, including roses, purple hazel and cornus, that add height and attractive background colours to the scene. In spring, one of the prettiest of backdrops is produced by a twisted old Judas tree (*Cercis siliquastrum*) bedecked with lilac-coloured flowers.

Left Carefully placed pots complement the planting and help to frame views.
Above The avenue of *Chamaecyparis lawsoniana* 'Fletcheri', described as 'pudding trees' by Margery Fish.

Sprinkled amongst cottage-garden favourites – both here and elsewhere in the garden – are unexpected beauties, such as *Lathyrus aureus*, an everlasting pea with golden-orange flowers. As Margery's knowledge grew, and following Walter's death in 1947, she was free to indulge her passion for small flowers. She loved hardy geraniums, astrantias, primroses and snowdrops and slowly built up a collection of lesser-known varieties. These were her 'treasured flowers' which, as cottagers had done for centuries, were added as and when they were acquired and 'wherever there was room'.

'I am afraid the cottages and their little gardens may disappear completely as the years go by and we shall have to remember them by the flowers,' Margery Fish wrote in *Cottage Garden Flowers* (1961). She did her bit to save many rare cottage garden plants, acquiring seeds and cuttings from neighbours and hunting out old varieties, including old forms of coloured primroses. And she started her own plant nursery in the late 1950s, having opened the garden to the public a few years earlier. Today it is a treasure trove of unusual cottage garden plants. Some, such as *Primula* 'Lambrook Mauve' and *Pulmonaria* 'Margery Fish', are named after the garden or its creator.

Above Margery Fish had a love of hardy geraniums; many varieties can still be seen growing in the garden today and are available to buy in the small on-site nursery. **Right** A sculptural cardoon presides over the silver garden. **Opposite** What could be prettier than a soft-pink rose clambering up a tree?

But back to our tour of the garden. Beyond the Terrace is a small triangular plot, made up of yet more narrow paths and changes in level. This is the southern end of the garden and the only area with relatively free-draining soil. It is the perfect hot spot for silver-leaved Mediterranean plants, from sculptural cardoons (*Cynara cardunculus*), wispy artemisias and tactile lamb's ears (*Stachys byzantina*) to dainty dianthus and spiky irises. Here the palette is more restricted: soft blues and purples (nepetas) and pinks (cistus) with a few added yellows (*Sisyrinchium striatum*) for added warmth and vibrancy. Interlaced throughout is one of Margery Fish's favourite plants, Sicilian honey garlic (*Nectaroscordum siculum*), its tall stems topped with clusters of cream and purple bells.

After such floral punch the garden offers a pause, with two quieter areas: a small White Garden, where in spring you can spot Margery's favourite double white primrose, and the Top Lawn, a patch of grass – the only one in the garden – adorned with the attractive sycamore, *Acer pseudoplatanus* 'Brilliantissimum'.

The atmosphere takes a dramatic turn as you follow the narrow path behind the Malthouse. Known as the Lido, this dark area is the haunt of rodgersias, skunk cabbages, *Darmera peltata* and other shade- and moisture-loving plants. Your steps follow a narrow gully whose banks are home to yet more hardy geraniums and aquilegias, but also euphorbias and swathes of *Gladiolus communis* subsp. *byzantinus*. Early in the year, it is a carpet of snowdrops, followed by candelabra primulas in spring.

Yet more snowdrops – there are over 150 different varieties in the garden – can be enjoyed in the Wooded Helleborus Garden. This is a magical mini-woodland, defined by subtle plays of dappled light, where small, elegant trees (*Acer griseum* and *Betula utilis* var. *jacquemontii*) combine with a year-round understorey of bulbs, perennials and shrubs.

As East Lambrook Manor's current owner Mike Werkmeister explains: 'The garden has been lucky. It has been well looked after since Margery Fish died in 1969.' Mike and his wife Gail took over in August 2008. Along with Head Gardener Mark Stainer, who has been working here for 45 years, he is passionate about preserving Margery Fish's legacy. But he never feels hidebound by it. 'If Margery Fish were alive today she would bring in new cultivars,' Mike explains. And so, like Margery, he and Mark are happy to introduce new plants here and there, watching the garden evolve over time, with no set plan.

There is no doubting that Margery would be pleased with how garden looks today, as it continues – half a century since her death – to embrace her famous mantra: 'When plants are allowed to grow naturally they make a harmonious picture and the result is a happy garden, and a happy garden is a peaceful one, with a backbone of plants that go on from year to year.'

Opposite One of the loveliest of all cottage garden flowers: the sweet pea. Above A tense tapestry of shade-loving plans growing at the back of the Malthouse. Left *Gladiolus communis* subsp. *byzantinus* and ox-eye daisies.

169

Cottage Gardens to Visit

Alfriston Clergy House
The Tye, Alfriston, Polegate, East Sussex BN26 5TL
www.nationaltrust.org.uk/alfriston-clergy-house

Anne Hathaway's Cottage
22 Cottage Lane, Shottery, Stratford-upon-Avon,
Warwickshire CV37 9HH
www.shakespeare.org.uk

Charleston Farmhouse
West Firle, Lewes, East Sussex BN8 6LL
www.charleston.org.uk

Coleridge Cottage
35 Lime Street, Nether Stowey, Bridgwater TA5 1NQ
www.nationaltrust.org.uk/coleridge-cottage

Dove Cottage
Grasmere, Cumbria LA22 9SH
www.wordsworth.org.uk

Dyffryn Fernant
Dinas, Fishguard, Pembrokeshire SA65 9SP
www.dyffrynfernant.co.uk

East Lambrook Manor Gardens
South Petherton, Somerset TA13 5HH
www.eastlambrook.com

The Garden at Elworthy Cottage
Elworthy, Taunton, Somerset TA4 3PX
www.elworthy-cottage.co.uk

Grafton Cottage
Barton-under-Needwood, Staffordshire DE13 8AL
www.ngs.org.uk (the NGS website has details of when
the garden is open)

Hardy's Cottage
Higher Bockhampton, near Dorchester, Dorset DT2 8QJ
www.nationaltrust.org.uk/hardys-cottage

Hilltop Garden
Woodville, Stour Provost, Gillingham, Dorset SP8 5LY
www.hilltopgarden.co.uk

Hill Top
Near Sawrey, Ambleside, Cumbria LA22 0LF
www.nationaltrust.org.uk/hill-top

Mary Arden's Farm
Station Rd, Wilmcote, Warwickshire CV37 9UN
www.shakespeare.org.uk

Monk's House
Rodmell, Lewes, East Sussex BN7 3HF
www.nationaltrust.org.uk/monks-house

Oakhurst Cottage
Hambledon, near Godalming GU8 4HF
www.nationaltrust.org.uk/oakhurst-cottage

Plas yn Rhiw
Rhiw, Pwllheli, Gwynedd LL53 8AB
www.nationaltrust.org.uk/plas-yn-rhiw

Rustling End Cottage
Codicote, Hertfordshire SG4 8TD
www.rustlingend.com

Smallhythe Place
Tenterden, Kent TN30 7NG
www.nationaltrust.org.uk/smallhythe-place

Townend
Troutbeck, Windermere, Cumbria LA23 1LB
www.nationaltrust.org.uk/townend

Weald and Downland Living Museum
Singleton, Chichester, West Sussex PO18 0EU
www.wealddown.co.uk

Right A pretty blend of linarias, penstemons and hardy geraniums.

Select Bibliography

Berridge, Vanessa, *Great British Gardeners*, Amberley Publishing, 2018

Dick, Stewart, *The Cottage Homes of England, Bracken Books*, 1991

Edwards, Ambra, *The Story of the English Garden*, National Trust, 2018

Fish, Margery, *An All the Year Garden*, Capital Books, 2001

Fish, Margery, *Carefree Gardening*, Faber & Faber, 1989

Fish, Margery, *Cottage Garden Flowers*, Batsford, 2016

Fish, Margery, *Gardening in the Shade*, Capital Books, 2001

Fish, Margery, *Ground Cover Plants*, Faber & Faber, 1980

Fish, Margery, *We Made a Garden*, Batsford, 2016

Hamilton, Geoff, *Geoff Hamilton's Cottage Gardens*, BBC Books, 1997

Hobhouse, Penelope, and Wood, Christopher, *Painted Gardens: English Watercolours 1850–1914*, Pavilion Books, 1988

Jekyll, Gertrude, *Old West Surrey*, 1904 (available to read online)

Keating, Honora M., *Plas yn Rhiw*, National Trust, 1982

Lacey, Stephen, *Gardens of the National Trust*, National Trust, 2016

Lloyd, Christopher and Bird, Richard, *The Cottage Garden*, Dorling Kindersley, 1999

Masset, Claire, *Beatrix Potter's Hill Top*, National Trust, 2016

Masset, Claire, *Virginia Woolf at Monk's House*, National Trust, 2017

Scott-James, Anne, *The Cottage Garden*, Penguin, 1982

Tinniswood, Adrian, *Life in the English Country Cottage*, Weidenfeld & Nicolson, 1995

Way, Twigs, *The Cottage Garden*, Shire Books, 2001

Willes, Margaret, *The Gardens of the British Working Class*, Yale University Press, 2015

Zoob, Caroline, *Virginia Woolf's Garden: The Story of the Garden at Monk's House*, Jacqui Small LLP, 2013

Picture Credits

Index

Acknowledgements

I would like to thank Peter Taylor and Katie Bond for commissioning me, Chris Lacey for his beautiful photography, Katie Hewett for her expert editing, Claire Clewley for her wonderful design, and my mum, Sarah, for her proofreading skills and unwavering moral support.

Thanks also to Darren Beatson at the National Trust Records and Archives for finding some very useful information on Oakhurst Cottage.

As ever I am hugely grateful to the gardeners and experts who have kindly answered my questions and patiently shown me round their lovingly tended plots: Carlotta Holt, Phil Loring, Caps Browning-Smith and the team at Hardy's Cottage, Llifon Jones, Glyn Jones, Pete Tasker, Mike Calnan, Tom Wells, Mike Werkmeister and Pete Keefe.

This book is dedicated to Alex, my long-suffering garden-visiting companion.

Right A haze of fennel and hollyhocks in late summer.